Life Course: Integrative Theories and Exemplary Populations

AAAS Selected Symposia Series

Published by Westview Press, Inc.
5500 Central Avenue, Boulder, Colorado

for the

American Association for the Advancement of Science
1776 Massachusetts Avenue, N.W., Washington, D.C.

Life Course: Integrative Theories and Exemplary Populations

Edited by Kurt W. Back

AAAS Selected Symposium **41**

AAAS Selected Symposia Series

This book is based on a symposium which was held at the 1979 AAAS National Annual Meeting in Houston, Texas, January 3-8. The symposium was sponsored by AAAS Sections H (Anthropology), K (Social and Economic Sciences), and L (History and Philosophy of Science), and by a AAAS affiliate, The Gerontological Society.

Published in 1980 in the United States of America by
  Westview Press, Inc.
  5500 Central Avenue
  Boulder, Colorado 80301
  Frederick A. Praeger, Publisher

Library of Congress Cataloging in Publication Data
Main entry under title:
Life course: integrative theories and exemplary populations.
    (AAAS selected symposium ; 41)
    Based on a symposium which was held at the 1979 AAAS national annual meeting in Houston, Texas, January 3-8, which was sponsored by the AAAS Section H (Anthropology) and others.
    Bibliography: p.
    Includes index.
    1. Life cycle, Human--Congresses. 2. Family life surveys--Congresses.
    I. Back, Kurt W. II. American Association for the Advancement of Science. Section on Anthropology. III. Series: American Association for the Advancement of Science. AAAS selected symposium ; 41.
HQ1059.4.L53   305   80-10917
ISBN 0-89158-777-2

Printed and bound in the United States of America

About the Book

In this interdisciplinary study of the human life course as a unit, scholars examine aspects of the life course, looking at several features over a short span and at a few traits over a longer period. Part 1 provides an overview from disciplines (e.g., history, demography, sociology) that are concerned with understanding the human life course; Part 2 contains studies of special populations in which integration of a variety of experiences over time can be accomplished. Based on these approaches, new methods appropriate to a science of human life are proposed and discussed in a form suitable for students, faculty, and professionals in human development (sociology, anthropology, psychology), demography, and gerontology.

About the Series

The *AAAS Selected Symposia Series* was begun in 1977 to provide a means for more permanently recording and more widely disseminating some of the valuable material which is discussed at the AAAS Annual National Meetings. The volumes in this *Series* are based on symposia held at the Meetings which address topics of current and continuing significance, both within and among the sciences, and in the areas in which science and technology impact on public policy. The *Series* format is designed to provide for rapid dissemination of information, so the papers are not typeset but are reproduced directly from the camera-copy submitted by the authors. The papers are organized and edited by the symposium arrangers who then become the editors of the various volumes. Most papers published in this *Series* are original contributions which have not been previously published, although in some cases additional papers from other sources have been added by an editor to provide a more comprehensive view of a particular topic. Symposia may be reports of new research or reviews of established work, particularly work of an interdisciplinary nature, since the AAAS Annual Meetings typically embrace the full range of the sciences and their societal implications.

WILLIAM D. CAREY
Executive Officer
American Association for
the Advancement of Science

Contents

Figures and Tables

xii   Figures and Tables

About the Editor and Authors

Kurt W. Back *is James B. Duke Professor of Sociology, chairman of the Department of Sociology, and professor of medical sociology at Duke University. His research has been in the field of social psychology, most recently in methodology and gerontology, and he has developed a simulation of the human life course for the National Institute on Aging. He is the author of many articles on methods of social research, encounter groups, population, self image, and the life course. He has written or edited a number of books, including* In Search for Community: Encounter Groups and Social Change *(AAAS Selected Symposium No. 4; Westview, 1978).*

Toni Antonucci *is assistant research scientist at the Institute for Social Research and an assistant professor in the Department of Family Practice, University of Michigan Medical School. A specialist in life-span developmental psychology, she has published on the topics of attachment as a life-course concept, values across three generations, role models in higher education, social support, and supports of the elderly.*

Denise Del Vento Bielby *is a lecturer at the University of California-Santa Barbara. She is a former fellow of the Institute of Human Development, University of California-Berkeley. She has studied cognitive functioning in adults and the elderly, moral functioning across the life span, and women's work cycle. Her specific area of specialization is life-span human development and adult development and aging, and she has been a recipient of a National Research Service Award for her work from the National Institute of Mental Health.*

Steven Dubnoff, *study director for the Center for Survey Research (Boston), works in the fields of historical and economic sociology. He has studied the family and work motiva-*

tion in an early industrial setting   and the changes in economic constraints on family life.

Tamara K. Hareven *is a research associate at the Center for Population Studies, Harvard University, and professor of history at Clark University. She has played a central role in the development of the field of family history and in interdisciplinary research on the family and the life course. She has written or edited several books in this field, among them* Transitions: The Family and the Life Course in Historical Perspective *(Academic, 1978) and* Family and Kin in American Urban Communities, 1780-1940 *(Franklin Watts, 1977). She is currently editor of the* Journal of Family History *and consulting editor to the* American Journal of Sociology.

Robert J. Havighurst, *professor emeritus of education and human development in the Department of Behavioral Sciences, University of Chicago, has studied human development through the life span with particular emphasis on gerontology and retirement. Among his numerous publications are* Adjustment to Retirement: A Cross-National Study *(Humanities Press, 1969) and* Social Scientists and Educators: Lives After 60 *(University of Chicago, Committee on Human Development, 1976).*

Barbara Myerhoff *is professor and head of the Department of Anthropology at the University of Southern California. A social anthropologist who has studied gerontology, religion, myth, and ritual, she is the author of numerous articles and books, including* Life's Career--Aging: Cross-Cultural Studies of Growing Old *(with Andrei Simic; Sage Press, 1977),* Changing Images of the American Family *(with V. Tufte; Yale University Press, 1979), and* Number Our Days *(Dutton, 1979). Her documentary film, "Number Our Days," (produced and directed by Lynne Littman) about an aged Jewish community in Southern California, won an Academy Award (1977) and is currently being dramatized for public television.*

James Olney *is a professor in the Department of English at North Carolina Central University. His field is English literature and he is the author of* Metaphors of Self: The Meaning of Autobiography *and* Tell Me Africa: An Approach to African Literature *(Princeton University Press, 1972 and 1973) and* The Rhizome and the Flower: The Perennial Philosophy--Yeats and Jung *(University of California Press, 1979), and the editor of* Autobiography: Essays Theoretical and Critical *(Princeton University Press, 1980).*

Pamela J. Perun *is a research associate at Wellesley College. She has studied adult development and aging, lifespan development, models of mid-life, and career development and patterns of retirement of women. She has received a*

National Research Service Award for her work from the National Institute of Mental Health.

Lois M. Tamir *is a research fellow in survey research at the Institute for Social Research of the University of Michigan. A developmental psychologist by training, she has studied the family life cycle, aging, mental health, and interpersonal interactions. She is the author of* Communication and the Aging Process: Interaction Throughout the Life Cycle *(Pergamon, 1980).*

Eleanor Walker Willemsen, *associate professor and head of the Department of Psychology at the University of Santa Clara, is a specialist in developmental psychology. She is the author of a number of articles on sex roles and differences and of a book,* Understanding Infancy *(Freeman, 1979).*

Halliman H. Winsborough *is a professor of sociology and a fellow of the Institute for Research on Poverty, University of Wisconsin. A former director of the Data and Computation Center and of the Center for Demography and Ecology of the University of Wisconsin, he has worked in the areas of social demography and related methodological issues. Since 1971 he has been editor of the Population Studies Series (Academic Press). His most recent book is* Analyzing Longitudinal Data: Age, Period and Cohort Effects *(coeditor with O. D. Duncan; Academic Press, 1980).*

Life Course: Integrative Theories and Exemplary Populations

Introduction

The study of social aspects of human development has made great strides in the last decade. This field has now become a self-conscious unit of social research. The combination of sociologists, psychologists and demographers looking at different aspects of human life and the confluence of interest in different phases of life, childhood, adolescence, adulthood, middle and old age, into one framework has sparked interest in human development as a process and led to new models and techniques.

The main advance, however, has been in the technical aspects of research. It has become possible to collect a number of data sets which represent the development of large parts of the population. The pure availability of large capacity computers has made it possible to process and analyze in detail the data sets and combined the advances in the design of data collection with analysis of data. Statements which were not even conceivable about the human life cycle a few decades ago can be made with confidence based on standard technique. Hypotheses about the influence of early experiences on later life or the distinctions between the influence of chronological age as such on an individual's life experience and membership in a particular cohort can be tested with sufficient and adequate sets of data.

The advance of knowledge has all the advantages and disadvantages of routinization. Great numbers of competent researchers have constructed, analyzed and re-analyzed a variety of data sets. Advanced techniques are available to many scientists and accumulations of accurate facts about the life cycle can be compared, discussed and codified. On the other hand, this new power of data handling may result in a routine of a great number of research projects designed for variables which are measurable according to accepted standards. This "normal science" approach would fill in missing data in

a current model but would by its very nature, restrict research
to facts and theories which can be handled by the techniques
designed for the large scale statistical survey.

It may be premature to say that the time has come for a
"scientific revolution" but it is fruitful in any case to
look for sources of new ideas. The recent advance has resulted
from the injection of large scale quantitative research into
fields which have traditionally used clinical, experimental
or case study approaches. If we want to avoid the fate of
extreme mechanization in which one study after another is
ground out with slight variations of questions or of populations
we ought to look at possible combinations with the approaches
which have been recently neglected, which stress the uniqueness
and personal meaning of the individual life course.

The collection of papers in this volume is dedicated to
making a start in this direction. The papers are organized
in two sections. One is the contribution of the different
disciplines in the humanities and social sciences which are
important in the study of the human life course and could
become even more so. There may be disagreement about the
value of interdisciplinary vs. disciplinary research (and some
papers disagree widely on this issue) but clearly an understanding of the possible contributions of other disciplines
can help anybody in finding new insights and ideas. The
study of the human life course is a search for systematical
regularities in events of unique meaning. We look at this
task with the intention of preserving the uniqueness, while
at the same time making general statements. This tension in
this field is vital but also makes it difficult and it is
incumbent on all of us to attempt to blend the procedure of
the humanist and the social scientist.

It is opportune, therefore, that the two essays representing humanistic discipline open the volume. These essays
sound two themes which recur in different forms through the
other essays in the volume. The first paper, by historian
Tamara Hareven, The Life Course in Historical Perspective,
raises as a point the importance of the measurement of absolute
time as milestones for the course of life. In some periods,
and societies, our own probably the most prominent, chronological age becomes the most important feature for judging events.
We know when a child is going to school, the normal time for
leaving home, for getting married, for retirement, etc. Thus,
using age as a comparison to measure how far one has gotten in
one's life comes naturally. In other societies, however, or
in other periods of time, age is less important than relationship to others. Leaving home, for instance, is a function of
birth order and sex; retirement in agricultural communities is

a question of the ages and needs of the children. In this
case it would be more fair to say that the sequence of events
becomes more important than the chronological age at which
they occur. The relative importance of order of events and of
chronological age, which are relevant in the life cycle and
of satisfaction with one's life, is one of the contributions
which the historian makes to the study of lives. In the
second essay, the biographer, James Olney, discusses the fact
that the unity of the human life course is imposed from the
outside and does not reflect the actual experience of the
person whose life is lived. He shows this in comparing the
essential features of biography and autobiography. Much of
the material which social scientists use are in effect autobiographical data, such as answers to questionnaires, interviews,
or tests of personality. In order to make the data conform to
a mass data analysis, the social scientist, in a sense, trans-
forms autobiographical into biographical data. The biographical
data then correspond to a certain scheme, framework, or
theory which an investigator might have. The contrast which
Olney shows in literary autobiography and biography becomes
important for a general analysis of the life course, imposing
order and sequence on events where none originally exist.
These two themes of the imposed order on subjectively disparate
events, and relativity of chronological age appear in the
papers which follow from different points of view.

     Fron the point of view of developmental psychology,
Antonucci et al. bridge psychology and history by studying
the historical context of individual happiness, of problems
at different stressful stages of life and the ways of coping
with them. They do this by using a follow-up study on mental
health of Americans after a 20 year interval. They show how
different groups have become satisfied, partly because of
social changes. Different times and stages in the life course
might be more critical and stressful than others. Thus, the
organization, the timing as well as the meaning of life depends
on the historical as well as social context.

     Representing demography, Hal Winsborough shows how rigorous
yet simple demographic techniques can show much about influences
on individuals by the immediate social situation. He gives as
a good example of his own position that much progress can be
made by sticking to one discipline, using the techniques and
letting the facts speak in a general concert of opinion. He
brings data which we have from different generations into
juxtaposition so we can find out any relationship between
parent and child which is, in effect, the environment in which
the child grows up. It becomes important, for instance, whether
the son has or is expected to have higher educational attainment
than his father. This had been so in the previous decade, but

is different now when the higher-educated older generation is gradually appearing. This one relationship alone, may lead to inferences about generational relationships and even generational complexities. One can imagine that a generation which cannot distinguish itself by education from its parents has to find other cultural ways of distinguishing itself. Thus the generation gap may be due to the fact that generations have become similar in many characteristics. The timing of one's life in comparison to one's parents and the meaning which norms and deviations give, can be constructed by the skill of the demographer.

A second way in which humanistic and social science approaches intersect is in the nature of the populations studied. Standards of social sciences put great emphasis on representative samples to give the picture of the whole society; the humanist typically studies the lives of exemplary individuals or groups. The second set of papers represents a merging of the two points of view, using the methods of the social scientist to study several unusual populations which may serve as examples for successful solutions to life's problems from career choices to retirement.

Two studies treat an example of retired social scientists and university administrators. Robert Havighurst discusses the male part of the sample and the patterns in which generally successful men have retired. There is probably as much of a variety of meanings as there are individual careers, but it was possible for Havighurst to group them into three different consistent patterns which give the individual meaning of living in a different population. Perun and Bielby deal with the female part of the same sample. The principal focus of their paper is to establish the importance of synchronicity of different fields of events. These women have one series of the academic career events, but in addition and running beside it are series of family events, marriage, children, etc. The paper proposes a theoretical model of dealing with the synchronicity and then tries to test the effect and conditions on different patterns of sequences and time effect. This paper shows how important sequences and relationships are, even in a society where age has become so important as a marker. It also shows ways to integrate meaningfully the different areas of life, career, family, community, intellectual development and to pull out the important patterns in which different events in each area can interact with one another.

Another group of unusual women, and also with superior intelligence, is studied by Willemsen. This group of women, which are generally known as the Terman Group of Gifted Children, have been followed up for over 50 years. Thus we

have the advantage of a long series of data. In this paper,
Willemsen studies the important events which the women perceived and then shows how the events can be used to organize
the lives and to establish different patterns.

Barbara Myerhoff uses a unique group of aged people maintaining a community in California. She shows how this group,
with a wealth of experiences, has given meaning to their life
histories. She demonstrates effectively how anthropological
techniques can teach the respondents themselves to give a
vivid picture of their lives, their experiences and their
values. By her ingenious methods of teaching them as a
community to produce their own life histories, she can combine
vividness and balance and also be helpful to the people with
whom she works.

The final paper summarizes the problem as a question of
language. Poets as well as mathematicians have been forced
to new styles to represent the complexity of the human life
course. Looking at methods and scientific discipline as
different languages, we can see the value of developing one's
own style and language as well as of developing a lingua
franca. Use of particular as well as universal language has
a place in research as well as literature. The right mix,
as represented in these papers, can lead us to the next step
in the study of the human life course.

Part 1

Disciplinary Approaches

1. The Life Course and Aging in Historical Perspective

The Life Course as an Interdisciplinary and Historical Concept

The interaction between individual development, collective family development and historical forces has only recently begun to attract scholars' attention. While the study of the individual life span has for some time commanded the attention of psychologists, and while family development has been the domain of sociologists, it is only recently that an effort to examine these processes in a historical context has begun to mature.

This essay discusses the potential of the life course approach for the understanding of this interaction between individual and collective family development and historical forces. It concludes with the proposal for a future agenda for the development of an historical phenomenology of the life course.

The emergence of the history of childhood and of the family has led historians to an exploration of developmental patterns in the past. Historians now recognize that "childhood," "adolescence" and other stages of the life cycle, particularly as formulated by Erikson (1946) were not just subject to different definitions and experiences in the past but also among different groups in a given historical

I am indebted to the National Institute on Aging for support under a Research Career Development Grant (#K04 AG00026-01), to the Center for Population Studies, Harvard University for its support and to Howard Litwak for editorial assistance.

population. Similarly, they recognize that stages of
the family cycle, particularly as defined by Hill (1970),
were subject to considerable variation under different
historical conditions. As a result, since it is clear
that childhood, adolescence, youth, adulthood, middle
age and old age were not constant over time, the process
of change in their respective definitions and experiences
under different historical conditions has become an important research subject. In studying it, historians
as well as psychologists and sociologists have begun to
discover the limitations of the life cycle and family
cycle for historical research, particularly in their
formulation of a priori stages, which do not always fit
the historical reality (Elder, 1978; Hareven, 1978).

The life course construct overcomes the shortcomings
of both the life cycle and the family cycle approach. It
examines the synchronization of individual behavior with
the collective behavior of the family unit, as each changes over time and in their interaction with external
historical conditions. Its essence is the interaction
between "individual time," "family time" and "historical
time." As Elder (1975, 1978) defines it, the life course
encompasses the "pathways" by which individuals fulfill
different roles over their lives, sequentially or simultaneously. In measuring the movement of individuals and
families from one role or status to the next, or the simultaneous balancing of roles, the life course concerns
itself with the process of transitions under different
historical conditions.

The life course approach is also interdisciplinary
by its very nature: its heritage combines several psychological, sociological and demographic traditions. It
draws on life history analysis, on life span psychology,
on the sociology of age differentiation, and on the concept of cohorts as developed by demographers.

I will now turn to three essential features of life
course analysis of particular significance to historical
analysis: 1) Timing, the synchronization of different
individual roles over a person's career, as well as the
synchronization of individual transitions with collective
family behavior; 2) interaction, the relationship between
life course transitions and historical changes; and 3) integration, the cumulative impact of earlier life course
transitions on subsequent ones.

The first feature is timing. The life course concerns
itself with two essential kinds of timing: 1) The timing

of transitions over an individual's career, particularly
the balancing of entry into and exit from different roles;
2) The synchronization of seemingly individual transitions
with those of other family members, and with transitions
which the entire family undergoes over its life. These
aspects of timing cannot be understood exclusive of their
interaction with external historical forces. For that
reason, the use of the term "timing" in a historical context requires a specific definition. Elder's definition
of timing as age-specific is relevant to a historical
setting but, as will be suggested below, in a historical
context, age was not the most critical aspect of timing
along the life course.

Individually, the crucial question is how people plan
and organize their lives and time their transitions. On
the non-familial level, entry into and exit from school
or the labor force and migration, or on the familial level,
leaving or returning home, marriage and setting up an independent household, are all subject to timing. Timing
also involves the synchronization of individual moves with
familial ones and familial transitions with non-familial
ones. For example, the extent to which taking a job is
related to leaving home, or the extent to which getting
married is linked with needs in one's family or orientation
are all subject to synchronization.

The metaphor which captures best the interrelation-
ship of individual transitions and changing family configurations is the movement of "schools of fish." As people
age, they group and regroup themselves in different configurations. The functions which they take on in these
clusters also vary significantly. Most individuals are
involved simultaneously in several family configurations,
fulfilling different functions in each. A married adult,
for example, is part of both a family of origin and a family of procreation (occupying a different position and
fulfilling a different role in each); in addition, such
an individual also figures in his or her spouse's family
of orientation, and in the spouse's kin network. When a
son leaves home, his departure changes the configuration
of his family unit. Depending on the status he held, his
family might find itself less one bread winner, or less
one dependent. When he marries and forms a new family
unit, his roles and obligations differ from the ones he
held in his parents' unit. This seemingly individual
move impinges upon the collective conditions of at least
three family units -- his family of origin, his newly
founded family and his wife's family of origin. In situations where remarriage follows death of a spouse or

divorce, the new spouse's family enters the orbit of relationships, while the former spouse's family does not necessarily disappear completely. In case of divorce for instance, a woman would stop relating to her former husband's
mother as her mother-in-law but may continue to relate to
her as her child's grandmother.

The second important feature of life course analysis
is the impact of historical processes on the timing of
individual or family transitions. Life course transitions are timed through the interaction of demographic,
social and economic factors, as well as under the influence of familial preferences. Demographic changes
in mortality, fertility and nuptiality affect the age
configurations within the family and the length of overlap among family members over their lifetime. Cultural
changes in norms of timing and economic changes in the
opportunity structure affect entry into the labor force,
job availability and ultimately retirement. Institutional and legislative changes such as compulsory school
attendance, child labor laws and mandatory retirement
affect entry into the labor force, job availability and
ultimately retirement.

The very question of cohort historical or social
changes in the life course requires more elaborate definition. "Historical change" is usually defined by non-
historians as macro-societal change, and as the impact
of one specific major event, such as the Great Depression
or the war. But actually, the important contribution
which historical research makes is in specifying and examining synchronic changes, which often have a more
direct impact on the life course than the macro ones.
Most importantly, historians can identify the convergence of socio-economic and cultural forces, which are
characteristic of a specific time period, and which
impinge directly on life course timing.

Ryder (1965) has suggested that social change occurs
when there is a distinct discontinuity between the experiences of one cohort and those of its predecessors. However, important historical discontinuities can also occur
within the same cohort. Intra-cohort variation is extremely significant for the understanding of social change.
Variations in exposure to events by class and community
background within each cohort would affect important differences between members of the same cohort.

This leads us to the third feature of life course
analysis: the cumulative impact of earlier transitions

on subsequent ones. A life course approach views a cohort
as an age group moving through history whose social experience is influenced not only by contemporary conditions but
also by its experience of earlier life course transitions.
This pattern can be grasped on two levels: 1) the direct
consequences of earlier life course experiences on subsequent development; 2) the experiences of a cohort at one
point in time as they relate to historical conditions
affecting its previous life course experiences. Elder's
Children of the Great Depression, one of the outstanding
studies addressing these questions, documents the impact
of Depression experiences in childhood and early adulthood
on subsequent adult experiences. Within the same cohort
of unemployed adults caught in the Great Depression,
coping with unemployment would have differed not only in
terms of the availability of other resources, personality
and family backgrounds, but also in terms of earlier transitional experiences -- how long the individual had been
working, whether his or her career had been continuous and
stable or had already been disrupted, and what historical
circumstances had affected such earlier discontinuities.

The life course framework thus offers a comprehensive,
integrative approach, which steers one to interpret individual and family transitions as part of a continuous
process of historical change, even if they are only observed at one point in time. It also helps one view an individual transition (leaving home or marriage, for example),
as part of a cluster of other concurrent transitions and
as part of a sequence of transitions affecting each other.
In short, the life course approach links individual biography with collective behavior as part of an ongoing continuum of historical change.

Historical Changes in the Timing of Life Course Transitions

The timing of life course transitions has changed
significantly in American society over the past two centuries (Hareven, 1977; Uhlenberg, 1978). Demographic,
economic and cultural factors have combined to account
for differences in the timing of such life transitions
as leaving home, entry into and exit from the labor force,
marriage, parenthood and post-parental stages and widowhood.

As Uhlenberg (1974, 1978) suggests, over the past
century several important demographic developments have
tended to effect greater uniformity in the life course of
American families, and have considerably increased the
chances for intact survival of the family unit over the

lifetime of its members. As a result of the decline in
mortality since the late nineteenth century, the chances
for children to survive into adulthood, and to grow up
with their siblings and both parents alive, have increased
considerably. Similarly, the chances for women to survive
till adulthood and to fulfill the script of marriage, raising of children jointly with a husband, and survival with
husband through the launching stage (Uhlenberg, 1974) have
increased steadily. For women, these changes, combined
with earlier marriage and earlier completion of maternal
roles, have meant a more extended period of life without
children in their middle years. At the same time, women's
tendency to live longer than men has resulted in a pro-
tracted period of widowhood in later years of life. Because of lower life expectancy and a greater tendency to
remarry in old age, men normally remain married until
death (Glick, 1977; Glick and Norton, 1977).

Historical investigation of cohorts of American women
from 1870 to 1930 has thus shown that an increasing proportion of the population has entered prescribed family
roles and, except for divorce, has lived out its life in
family units (Uhlenberg, 1974). Contrary to conventional
assumptions, the American population has thus experienced
an increasing uniformity in family cycle life course transitions. (The recent increase in solitary residence since
the 1950's suggests a change in the pattern [Kobrin, 1976]).

Curiously, the demographic factors responsible for
these continuities have also, over the past century, gen-
erated discontinuities in the timing of such life course
transitions as movement into and out of family roles and
work roles. Here they are closely related to the gradual
segmentation of the life course into societally acknowledged
stages: childhood, youth, adolescence, adulthood, middle
age, and old age (Kett, 1977; Hareven, 1976; Fischer, 1977;
Keniston, 1971; Neugarten, 1968). The most significant
expression of such discontinuities had been in the timing
of the complex of activities involved in making the transition to adulthood, especially leaving home, marriage,
family formation and parenthood. As Modell, Furstenberg
and Hershberg have shown (1976), age uniformity in the
timing of such transitions has become increasingly more
marked and the transitions have been more rapidly timed
and abrupt. In the nineteenth century the time in which
a cohort accomplished such transitions varied. In the
twentieth century, transitions to adulthood have become
more uniform, orderly in sequence and definitive. The
very notion of embarking on a new stage, and the implications of movement from one stage to the next, has become

more generally recognized.

Two important discontinuities have emerged in the middle and later years of life: the "empty nest" in a couple's middle age and mandatory retirement in their old age. The combination of earlier marriage and fewer children overall, segregation of childbearing to the early stages of the family cycle and children's more uniformly leaving home earlier in their parents' lives, has resulted in a more widespread emergence of the empty nest as a characteristic of middle and old age (Glick, 1977). In the nineteenth century, later age at marriage, higher fertility, and shorter life expectancy rendered different family configurations from those characterizing contemporary society. Thus, for large families, the parental stage, with children remaining in the household, extended over a longer period of time, sometimes over the parent's entire life.

Since children in families were spread along a broad age spectrum younger children could observe their older siblings and near relatives moving through adolescence and into adulthood. Older siblings in turn trained for adult roles by acting as surrogate parents for younger siblings. Only a small number of adults lived alone, and the family as well as the larger society experiences a greater integration among age groups.

In contemporary society, by contrast, the postparental period comprises one-third or more of the married adult life span (Glick, 1977). Glick concludes that the period of the empty nest has increased over the past eighty years by eleven years (from 1.6 years to 12.3 years): "The couple now entering marriage has the prospect of living together 13 years without children or more than one-third of the 44 years of married life that lay ahead of them at the time of marriage" (Glick, 1977:9). Growing sex differentials in mortality above age fifty have dramatically increased the ratio of females to males and have made widowhood a more important facet of women's lives. Uhlenberg (1978) has noted that the major change since the late nineteenth century has not so much been in the emergence of an empty nest but rather in the proportion of a woman's lifetime that this stage encompasses.

These developments are related in a larger context to the segmentation of the life course into specific developmental stages. This process has involved the gradual societal recognition of new stages of life and their integration into the experience of everyday life.

It became publicly recognized through the passing of legislation and the establishment of public institutions and
agencies for the realization of the potential of people
at a specific stage of life and for their protection within those stages. To the extent that it is possible to reconstruct a historic model, it appears that the "discovery"
of a new stage of life is itself a complex process. First,
individuals become aware of new characteristics in their
private experience. The articulation of such a stage and
of the conditions unique to it is then formulated by the
professionals, and eventually recognized in the popular
culture. Finally, if the conditions peculiar to this
stage seem to be associated with a major social problem,
it attracts the attention of public agencies, and its needs
and problems are dealt with in legislation and in the establishment of institutions. Those public activities in
turn affect the experience of individuals going through
such a stage, and clearly influence the timing of transitions in and out of such a stage.

In American society childhood was "discovered" first
in the private lives of middle class urban families in the
early part of the nineteenth century. The discovery itself
was related to the retreat of the family into domesticity,
the segregation of the work place from the home, the re-
definition of the mother's role as the major custodian of
the domestic sphere and the emergence of sentiment as the
basis of familial relationships. The new child-centered-
ness of urban domestic families in the early nineteenth
century was also a response to two major demographic
changes: a decline in infant and child mortality and an
increase in the conscious practice of family limitation.
After it emerged in the lives of middle class families,
childhood as a distinct stage of development became the
subject of the voluminous body of child-rearing and family
advice literature. This literature popularized the concept of childhood and the needs of children, prescribed
the means to allow them to develop as children and called
for the regulation of child labor.

The discovery of adolescence followed a similar
pattern. While puberty in itself is a universal, biological process, the psychosocial phenomena of adolescence
were only gradually defined, most notably by Stanley G.
Hall (1904) in the later part of the nineteenth century.
The experience of adolescence itself, particularly some
of the problems and tensions associated with it, was
apparent in the private lives of people reaching puberty
during the second half of the nineteenth century. The
congregation of young people in peer groups, and the symp-

toms of what might be characterized as a "culture of adolescence," were also observed by educators and urban re-
formers from the middle of the nineteenth century on.
Anxiety over such behavior increased particularly where
it was connected with new immigrants. Adolescence as a
new stage of life was articulated in the work of psychologists, particularly by Hall and his circle, and was
also widely popularized in the literature. The extension
of school age through high school, in the second part of
the nineteenth century, the further extension of the age
limits for child labor and the establishment of both ju-
venile reformatories and vocational schools, were all
part of the public recognition of the needs and problems
of adolescence.

The boundaries between childhood and adolescence on
the one hand, and between adolescence and adulthood on
the other, become more clearly demarcated during the
twentieth century. In fact, as Keniston (1971) has suggested, the extension of a moratorium from adult responsibilities beyond adolescence has resulted in the emergence of another stage, youth. However, despite the
growing awareness of these pre-adult stages, no clear
boundaries on adulthood in America emerged until "old
age" became prominent as a new stage of life, and with
it, the need to differentiate the social and psychological problems of "middle" from "old" age. The overall boundaries of adulthood are not yet sharply defined,
and the transitions into middle age are still fuzzy.
"Old age," though, is now recognized as a specific period
of adulthood. On the public level it has a formal beginning -- age 65, at least where an individual's working life is concerned, and it is institutionalized by
a rite of passage -- retirement and eligibility for social security (Fischer, 1977; Hareven, 1976).

The important connection between historical development and the emergence of such new stages has not
been fully documented. The general contours of the
pattern are, however, beginning to emerge with some
clarity. Whether childhood, adolescence, youth, middle
or old age were first experienced on the private, individual level, or acknowledged on the public, collective level, their very appearance and increasing societal recognition have affected the timing of family
transitions in the past. Thus not only the very experience of these stages of life has changed over time,
but also, the timing of people's entry into such stages
and exit from them, and the accompanying roles involved
in such timing have changed as well.

The existential as well as the institutional changes
which have buttressed the extension of a moratorium from
adult responsibilities have also affected the timing of
both individual and familial transitions. Thus, the post-
ponement of the assumption of adult responsibilities would
have meant longer residence of children in the household
without contributing to the family's economic effort, and
a resulting increase in the state of "dependency" or "semi-
dependency" as a typical experience of adolescence. On
the other end, the recognition of old age as a distinct
stage, and especially its imposition of discontinuity in
the form of mandatory retirement, has had a serious impact
on the timing of transitions in the family economy, leading to the emergence of dependency or semi-dependency in
old age, and imposing severe tensions and demands on family
obligations.

Familial Timing and Changing Life Course Patterns

The family was the central arena, in which many of
the aspects of timing were converging. This is the result of several important historical factors, which are
essential for our understanding of the difference between
past and present.

Many of the transitions which we would consider today
as individual, were, in the past, considered familial.
Even if they involved strictly individual activity, such
as the work life, they still impinged on at least several
other family members. Marriage, for example, was not
simply an individual or couple act, but rather one involving the alliance between families, the organization or
realignment of kinship ties and allegiances and the transfer of obligations from one family unit to another (Hareven, 1977).

The family also played a major role as the focus of
most important economic and welfare functions. This
central role for the family continued even after the separation of the work place from the home, and after the
transfer of many of the family's earlier educational and
social control functions to other institutions, following
the onset of industrialization. Despite the growing tendency of middle class urban families to retreat from the
outside world and to concentrate on domesticity and child
nurture as their exclusive role, the majority of families
continued to function as economic, or even work units.
Families and individuals relied heavily on kin relations
as their social safeguard. Timing was a critical factor
in the family's efforts to balance the contributions and

needs of different members to the family economy, especially during critical life situations. The multiplicity of obligations which individuals incurred over their life course was more complex than in the present regime of the welfare state, where such responsibilities are carried primarily by public agencies. This is not to say that at present kin do not continue to fulfill such obligations, but the division of responsibility is more clearly structured and differentiated (Hareven, 1978). The family was the most critical agent, both in initiating as well as in absorbing the consequences of transitions among individual members. Clearly, when viewed from this perspective, the essential aspect of the _timing_ of a transition was not the _age_ at which it occurred, but rather how it was related to those which other family members were undergoing.

The status of older people was clearly affected by the presence or absence of children or other young kin; conversely, the departure of children from the home was affected by parental needs in the household. Children who under other circumstances would have left home, remained with parents who needed support in old age. Interdependence in a familial setting imposed demands as well as constraints on timing that involved balancing a number of roles. The area of possible tension was even greater if one takes into consideration the conflict between two sets of norms: those governing internal obligations and expectations of mutual assistance among family members on the one hand, and those governing the appropriate age for the timing of transitions on the other.

This dilemma was the result of conflict between two different tendencies in American culture: one was the expectation that the integrity of the family of orientation be preserved. The other was the expectation that young adults achieve autonomy as soon as possible and carve their own place in the world. How were individuals able to fulfill both of these expectations? How could they become independent adults who headed their households and cared for their own children, and at the same time, also continue support of their family of orientation, especially for their aging parents?

The commitment to the nuclearity of the household in American culture made such choices even more difficult. Throughout the nineteenth century, residence in nuclear households seems to have been the norm. Interestingly, while there was a general opposition to extended kin in the household, there was a greater tolerance for strangers living in the household as boarders and lodgers. The com-

mitment to nuclearity of the household, strong for all
ethnic groups, had in itself important implications for
timing: the avoidance of extended family residence clearly required the establishment of an independent household
simultaneously with marriage. Children stayed longer in
their parental home, or, having left home, lived as boarders and lodgers in other people's households, until they
could afford an independent household.

In the absence of adequate public and institutional
means of support, older people were caught in the conflict
between having to rely on the continued support of their
children and the commitment to living in nuclear households. An analysis of late nineteenth century family
patterns suggests that generally, older people struggled
to retain the headship of their own households (Chudacoff
and Hareven, 1978).

The rule of the nuclearity of the household was most
likely to be broken or stretched during parents' dependency in old age, or during apparent housing shortages which
made it more difficult for newlyweds to afford separate
housing. Children either returned home with their spouses
to live with their aging parents, or, most often, the
youngest daughter postponed marriage, in order to continue
supporting older parents. The most common pattern was
that of children staying in their parents' household,
rather than parents moving in with their children. Even
older widows, generally the most vulnerable, continued to
hold on to the headship of their household as long as they
could. If there were no children available or able to
help, they took in boarders and lodgers. If they were
unable to continue to head their household, they, more
than widowed men, eventually had to move into the households of kin or strangers.

There is some indication that in a late nineteenth
century setting, the norms of familial assistance and
autonomy seemed to prevail over age norms of timing. This
is an area where the historical difference with our times
is dramatic. Life course transitions in contemporary society have become more strictly age-related, and more
rigidly governed by age-norms. Neugarten's definition
of being "late" or "on time" (1968) in one's fulfillment
of certain age-related roles reflects the standards of
age-norm bound society, while in earlier time periods,
economic needs and familial obligations prevailed over
age norms. The increasing trend towards specific age-
related transitions, which is characteristic of contemporary society, is thus closely related to the decline

in instrumental relations of kin over the past century.
This trend has led to the isolation of the elderly and
to increasing age segregation in American society.

Agenda: An Historical Phenomenology of the Life Course

The historical reconstructions of life course patterns
discussed so far have been limited to the behavioral level.
A historical reconstruction of life course phenomenology,
however, is still in its very beginnings. One of the
great values of following a life course approach is in
identifying conscious choices and priorities which individuals may have exercised in the timing of their life
course transitions.

The historical evidence has also shown that age as
such was not the critical factor in the timing of life
course transitions. More significant than age was the
sequence or coincidence in which transitions were expected to occur. Modell et al. (1976) have also shown that
even though nineteenth-century transitions to adulthood
were more flexible than today, they nevertheless generally
followed an established sequence: marriage followed the
departure from one's parental home and was conditioned on
the establishment of a separate household and of a means
of support. There seems to have been a preference for
keeping sons at home longer, while marrying off daughters
earlier, except for the youngest daughter, who was usually
expected to postpone her marriage and remain at home in
order to support aging parents. A number of other strategies of timing can be constructed by inference (Hareven, 1978).

A far more ambitious goal in understanding life
course patterns would be to reconstruct what Hughes (1971)
defines as "the moving perspective in which the person
sees his life as a whole and interprets the meaning of
his various attributes, actions and the things which
happen to him." In a historical context, this would
require an understanding of the interaction between an
individual's subjective life career and the collective
societal norms and expectations of behavior and roles at
different points in the life course and under different
historical conditions. To achieve this, we would need
to establish what the overall norms of timing were in a
society at specific points in time, how conscious individuals were of these norms and to what extent they took
them into account in the choices which they were making.
As LeVine (1978) puts it, "the focus of interest is how
people make sense of their lives with ideas drawn from

their cultural environment, what kind of order they find there, and how they are affected by conclusions they draw from their culturally guided introspection." An important aspect of this inquiry is the issue of a life plan. To what extent did individuals and families have such a plan; what were its major components, how was it in turn influenced by cultural values and social needs and how was it realized or frustrated in practice?

Historians have not yet embarked on a sytematic phenomenological exploration of the life course because of the lack of availability of appropriate data. But even where some historical sources which are valuable for this purpose have survived, they have not been exploited systematically for a deeper understanding of people's perceptions of their life course in the past. Prior to the emergence of the "new" social history, individual biography was one of the major pillars for the reconstruction of lives in the past. The sources which individual biographies are based on, namely letters, diaries, autobiographies, and, at times, interviews, could be utilized creatively in the reconstruction of the life course in the past. The problem is greater, however, if one wants to depart from a model of individual biography and reconstruct, instead, the experience of larger numbers of otherwise anonymous people. To fulfill this goal, the "new" social history using demographic sources, has reconstructed and aggregated family and occupational patterns, and to some extent also life course patterns for large numbers of people in the past (Hareven, 1978; Hareven and Vinovskis, 1978). While this approach has considerably expanded our historical knowledge, it has not, so far, provided us with the means to retrieve "mentalite" systematically.

More recently, we have begun to identify oral history as one of the important avenues toward the reconstruction of phenomenology. I have suggested elsewhere (Hareven, 1978) the advantages and pitfalls in the uses of oral history. Like the retrospective narratives patterned by anthropologists for contemporary populations, oral history might become one of the very few useful sources providing insight into how people felt about their life course and how they perceived their activities. To provide us with an effective linkage between perception and behavior, an analysis utilizing oral history must also be grounded in factual behavioral data. The ideal merger is between individual oral history narratives and life histories reconstructed from demographic data. Such a combination not only offers important checks on oral narratives, but also juxtaposes two different levels of a multilayered historical reality, offering an understanding of why behavior may have differed from perception.

Since the essence of life course analysis is an understanding of behavior over one's life rather than at an isolated point in time, any successful historical explanation of the life course is contingent on longitudinal data. The type of data from the Berkeley Human Development Study which Elder has used so imaginatively for his work, are not available for earlier time periods. To overcome this deficiency, some of us have attempted to construct longitudinal data sets for certain communities for the nineteenth and early twentieth centuries, and others have tried to infer longitudinal patterns from cross sectional data. Despite the limitations and shortages in data, we have not come close yet to exploring the existing data, nor have we even attempted yet to utilize creatively the treasury of existing longitudinal data sets. The historical study of aging from a life course perspective is actually very much on the frontier of historical research. As suggested above, a great deal of research is still required for the reconstruction of longitudinal patterns of behavior. Two other major dimensions that have been barely touched, namely, the phenomenological and the biological, invite systematic research. In their application of the life course to past populations, historians have greatly benefited from the conceptual and methodological contributions of sociology, psychology and economics. In their turn, historians can now make conceptual contributions to other social sciences.

A historical perspective, rather than merely documenting change, tries to get at the question of the meaning of change and at the ways in which individuals and families dealt with change in their own lives. In these respects, the historical study of the life course fulfills a function similar to that of cross-cultural studies in anthropology providing a comparative perspective with another culture.

Citations

Elder, Glen H., Jr.
    1975   "Age Differentiation and the Life Course." In
            Annual Review of Sociology, vol. 1, chap. 2.
            Palo Alto, California: Annual Reviews.

Erikson, Erik H.
    1946   "Ego Development and Historical Change." In
            The Psychoanalytic Study of the Child, vol. II,

359-396. New York: International Universities
Press.

Fischer, David H.
1977   Growing Old in America. New York: Oxford
University Press.

Glick, Paul C.
1977   "Updating the Life Cycle of the Family." Journal
of Marriage and the Family 39 (February): 5-13.

Glick, Paul C., and Arthur J. Norton
1977   "Selected Data from 'Marrying, Divorcing and
Living Together in the U.S. Today.'" Prepared
for Family Economic Behavior Seminar. American
Council on Life Insurance.

Hall, Stanley G.
1954   Adolescence: Its Psychology and its Relations
to Anthropology, Sociology, Sex, Crime, Religion,
Education. (2 volumes). New York: Appleton.

Hareven, Tamara K.
1976   "The Last Stage: Historical Adulthood and
Old Age." Daedalus (Fall): 13-27.

1977   "Family Time and Historical Time." Daedalus
(Spring): 13-27.

Hareven, Tamara K., ed.
1978   Transitions: The Family and the Life Course
in Historical Perspective. New York: Academic
Press.

Hareven, Tamara K.
1978   "The Dynamics of Kin in an Industrial Community."
American Journal of Sociology 84, Supplement,
1978.

Hareven, Tamara K., and Maris Vinovskis, eds.
1978   Family and Population in Nineteenth Century
America. Princeton, N.J.: Princeton University Press.

Hill, Reuben
1970   Family Development in Three Generations.
Schenkman: Cambridge.

Hughes, Everett C., ed.
1971   "Cycles, Turning Points and Careers." In The

Sociological Eye, Chicago: Aldine-Atherton.
vol. I: 124-131

Keniston, Kenneth
1971   "Psychological Development and Historical Change."
         Journal of Interdisciplinary History 2 (Autumn):
         329-345.

Kett, Joseph
1977   Rites of Passage: Adolescence in America, 1790
         to the Present. New York: Basic Books.

Kobrin, Frances E.
1976   "The Fall in Household Size and the Rise of the
         Primary Individual in the United States." Demo-
         graphy 13 (February): 127-138.

Levine, Robert A.
1978   "Comparative Notes on the Life Course." In
         Transitions: The Family and the Life Course in
         Historical Perspective, Tamara K. Hareven, ed.,
         287-296. New York: Academic Press.

Modell, J., Furstenberg, F, and Hirshberg, F.
1976   "Social Change and Transitions to Adulthood in
         Historical Perspective," Journal of Family
         History 1, 7 .

Neugarten, Bernice L., ed.
1968   Middle Age and Aging: A Reader in Social Psycho-
         logy. Chicago: University of Chicago Press.

Ryder, Norman
1965   "The Cohort as a Concept in the Study of Social
         Change." American Sociological Review 30: 843-
         861.

Uhlenberg, Peter
1974   "Cohort Variations in Family Life Cycle Experi-
         ences of U.S. Females." Journal of Marriage and
         the Family 34: 284-292

1978   "Changing Configurations of the Life Course."
         In Tamara K. Hareven, ed., Transitions: The Family
         and the Life Course in Historical Perspective.
         New York: Academic Press.

2. Biography, Autobiography and the Life Course

To a hasty eye, autobiography and biography look much
the same; to an inattentive ear, they can sound quite alike;
and to a superficial understanding, they may seem to be
writing performances that are indistinguishable one from
another. When one sees life (bios) and writing (graphé)
coupled, the temptation is - or with many observers has been -
to disregard the seemingly innocent four-letter prefix that
distinguishes the two words and the two practices and to
suppose that "for all practical purposes" they are one and the
same art or preoccupation or obsession or whatever it is to be
called. But the truth is the "auto-" is no more innocent than
many another four-letter word and the consequences of
attaching it to "biography" are very far from being incon-
sequential. What I would suggest is that the presence or
absence of "auto-" at the beginning of the hybrid word is
absolutely crucial for the sense of bios that determines
either and both of the acts. And bios, as a Greek lexicon
will tell us, means "the course of a life," so it is a word
not without relevance and interest in the present context of
discussions of "the life course." It should be remarked,
however, that a subtle but immensely important change in
meaning occurs when we pass from "the course of a life" to
"the life course." To this change of meaning I will return
later after some speculations on the radical differences
separating the act of biography from the act of autobiography.

The most brilliant phrase I know distinguishing the
different - indeed contrary - practices of biography and
autobiography comes in a letter of 1908 from Henry Adams to
his old friend Henry James, a letter accompanying a copy of
The Education of Henry Adams and describing that book: "The
volume is a mere shield of protection in the grave," Adams
wrote. "I advise you to take your own life in the same way,
in order to prevent biographers from taking it in theirs."
That Henry James followed Adam's advice and took his own life

in A Small Boy and Others and in Notes of a Son and Brother
has not, of course, prevented subsequent biographers from
taking his life in their ways. But the point is brilliantly
made all the same. "I advise you to take your own life"
before someone else takes it: autobiography as a pre-emptive
counter to biography, suicide as a prevenient preventative of
homicide. To another correspondent, but some seventeen years
earlier (that is, well before he "took his own life" in the
Education), Adams wrote to much the same effect: "The moral
seems to be that every man should write his own life, to
prevent some other fellow from taking it." Was Adams being
merely hyperbolical in his phrasing? I don't think so; and
the number of men - especially writers of one sort or another
- who have insisted that no one was to write their biography
would seem to suggest that others have felt much the same
hostility as Adams felt about being "biographed."

But why is it that so many men have been loath to have
their lives written down? Do they fear that shameful secrets
will be revealed, or that some hidden area of inner privacy
will be violated? These answers may in some instances
provide partial explanations, but both lose much of their
force when the biography proposed is to be written, as is the
usual case, after the subject's death. As Adams said, his
Education was designed as a "shield of protection in the
grave," and this provides a clue to why writers in particular
are reluctant to offer their lives (after death) as matter
for someone else's book. Like Adams they have already taken
their lives and they have written them out at large in their
works already - written them out in other characters than
those of biography but with a greater fidelity to inward truth
than documentary evidence can ever yield for the biographer.
T.S. Eliot (and others have done the same) stipulated in his
will that there was to be no authorized biography of his life,
and the logic of his refusal I think is clear: he had taken
his life previously by writing a spiritual autobiography in
his poetry. For someone else to write a biography, authorized
or not, after the poet's death would be a mere falsification
and an impertinence.

John Henry Newman was as reluctant as Henry Adams or
T.S. Eliot or any other writer to have someone else take his
life and the implicit reasons for his reluctance are very much
to the point. In the Grammar of Assent, speaking of what he
terms "real" and "notional" apprehensions and propositions,
Newman writes: "All things in the exterior world are unit and
individual, and are nothing else; but the mind not only
contemplates those unit realities, as they exist, but has the
gift, by an act of creation, of bringing before it abstractions
and generalizations, which have no existence, no counterpart,

out of it."   This is what the mind is capable of, and what it
does, with those "unit realities" that are individual lives,
and the abstraction or generalization that the mind, "by an
act of creation," brings before itself is what we are calling
"the life course" - which, as Newman says, has "no existence,
no counterpart, out of / the mind/."   The chief sin of most
biographers is that they do not (cannot) see the life, the
bios, from within as real life, a "unit reality," but are
condemned to view it from without as the life course, an
abstraction and a generalization.   Can anyone wonder that
Newman - or Adams or Eliot - should have been unwilling to
trade an existent reality, delicately realized in however many
volumes of poetry and autobiography, for an unreal abstraction
and a generalization that has no existence outside a
biographer's mind?   (I should emphasize again that I am
talking in particular about writers and not about, for example,
political figures or movie stars, whose lives are led in
public and who, for one reason and another, are avid to be
biographical subjects.   Their lives are in a sense "notional"
anyway so that a biography that presents them "notionally"
would be no falsification.)

    Consider, in this regard, the transfer of life that
occurs by a seemingly natural and deep-rooted linguistic
convention when a life is written and when "auto-" does not
stand at the head of the word designating the act of writing.
"Jones is writing the life of Smith": the expression is very
common and seems to cause no uneasiness or alarm (although one
can imagine Adams's reaction).   And the expression is acceptable whether Smith is still living the life in question or has
finished it, and is moreover acceptable whether Smith has
himself taken his life already or has failed to take it.   And
when the life of Smith has become The Life of Smith, do we not
conventionally transfer right, title, and interest in that
life to Jones - "Jones's life (or Life) of Smith"?   It is
"Jones's life" now, and that it is "of Smith" is not at all a
fact of sufficient force to return the life to its original
possessor.   I have quoted elsewhere the first instance known
to me of this linguistic appropriation of a life: it occurs
in Plutarch's "Life of Theseus" when Plutarch refers casually
but with assurance to "the writing of my parallel lives."   One
seems to hear, even as Plutarch deploys the dative of
possession to claim the lives for himself (emoi: "to me, for
me, therefore my lives"), an eerie, muffled cry coming from
beneath the text as Theseus tries to protest against his life's
being taken from him.   But the terrible irony, for Theseus
anyway, is that his unhappy cry will be forever muffled and
strangled because the only person possessed of speech in the
Parallel Lives is the author, the biographer, and Theseus has
been condemned for going on nineteen centuries now to listen

to us referring to Plutarch's life (of whom? Oh yes, of
Theseus, to be sure; but that is only a trailer to the real
possessive and possessor: "Plutarch's life"). And when
Jones finishes his work on Smith, Smith will in his turn
suffer the same unhappy fate as Theseus.

The biographer occupies a position somewhere between the
autobiographer, for whom life (to adopt Newman's terms again)
is real and ipso facto unique, and the social scientist, for
whom life is notional and general, a matter not of poignantly
individual experience but of norms and stages, statistics and
averages. Elsewhere in the Grammar of Assent, referring to
Elias and his exemption from death, Newman says that he would
have fallen under the rule that "all men are mortal" only if
he had been abstract man ("Man as a typical, abstract
creature is mortal; Elias was the abstract man; therefore..."),
but he "was not /abstract man/ and could not be such, nor
could any one else, any more than the average man of an
Insurance Company is every individual man who insures his life
with it." It is the crucial fact for autobiography that no
man conceives of himself as "the average man of an Insurance
Company" or of his experience as something that can be
adequately expressed by charts and graphs and tables. To so
conceive of himself and his experience would be to let the
Insurance Company take his life in its way, a folly a good
deal worse than letting a biographer take it in his way. "For
such as these," James Joyce once remarked of the artist who
would insist on being responsible for limning his own
portrait, "For such as these a portrait is not an identifi-
cative paper but rather the curve of an emotion," and there
is all the difference in the world between "the curve of an
emotion," the most delicate representation of the deepest
lyrical reality, and the actuarial curve of the life course
that might be plotted on a graph for purposes of determining
life insurance premiums.

The divergence of biography and autobiography is largely
a consequence of the writer's perspective and of the pattern
that is itself to a great degree determined by perspective,
for if you change perspective on one and the same subject -
in this case a certain life - the pattern discerned will
inevitably change as well. However determined he may be and
however sympathetic toward his subject, the biographer sees
from outside and observes a life that is - at least for his
purposes - finished and entire; in contrast, however
determined he may be and however "objective" in looking on his
earlier life, the autobiographer sees from inside, from within a moment of the life he recounts, and he observes a life
that cannot be finished and entire so long as this very act
of autobiography continues. In his "Autobiographical Notes"

Einstein makes the accurate observation, with regard to the act of autobiography, that "an individual in retrospect sees a uniformly systematic development, whereas the actual experience takes place in kaleidoscopic particular situations." The "uniformly systematic development" is of course a development towards, and hence is determined by the nature of, what the individual presently is. That is to say, the moment of being out of which the autobiographer writes is responsible for shaping the patterns of uniformly systematic development that he discerns or imagines himself to discern. Now is this in any way different from the practice of biography where, as readers, we certainly expect to be presented with a clear pattern and moreover a uniformly systematic one? In fact, I believe it is quite different and the reason is that each of us sees the lives of others as conforming to probabilities and as moving along the normalized curve plotted by those points that are the stages of life - this is how we see others' lives, but none of us sees his own life this way. Predictions can be made for the lives of others and probability obtains in those lives, but neither prediction nor probability has place in our own experience. To return to a distinction briefly glanced at earlier, the individual who "in retrospect sees a uniformly systematic development" is seeing the course of a life and is seeing bios in the lexical sense, but he is not seeing the life course nor is he seeing an abstraction derived from shuffling together statistics and averages. A biographer can tell us that "X did thus and so because he was then passing through the mid-life crisis," but this is not the explanation X would himself implicitly give; X would say that he did thus and so because he was on his way to becoming what he now is. This, as I say, is more a matter of the course of a life than of the life course and autobiography is typically motivated by its perception of the former, biography by its perception of the latter.

What joins the autobiographer to his subject and makes for an unfailing bond between what he is now and what he describes himself as having been earlier is memory. The faculty of memory, as we all know, differs from individual to individual, and indeed the kind of memory that an individual possesses - the kind of memory that informs his entire sense of his own past - can be taken as an important index of his specific personality or character. We remember, as it were helplessly, according to what we are, and what we are depends, to a large extent, on what and how we remember. Why do we remember some things and not others? Who can say? But this one thing is certain: that there is a creative, reciprocal and circular relationship between what we remember (or what we forget) and what we are, the one perpetually shaping the other and being simultaneously shaped by the other. Everyone is aware that memory can be the faultiest of human faculties,

but it can also be as creative as it is faulty. We remember
in the present and in so doing "recreate" the past - that is,
create it anew; but this past that has been recreated so that
it exists not as the past but as the present obviously has
great power to shape both present and future reality for us.
It cannot be strongly enough emphasized that memories, which
give shape to the autobiographer even as he gives shape to
them, are of the nature not of abstractions and generalizations
but of Newmanesque "unit realities." In remembering, one
experiences not the life course but life itself. Even when
the autobiographer has recourse to documents - letters,
diaries, notes - and seems to be availing himself of the same
materials as the biographer, there is still this difference:
that those documents are surrounded and suffused for him (as
they are not for the biographer) with memories of the time
when, the people with whom, and the situation in which they
came into being. Memory, which is essential to most autobiography, has little or nothing to do with most biography,
and thus the radical difference, both epistemological and
ontological, between the two modes.

   In The Principles of Psychology, William James presents
an illustrative little drama that nicely characterizes this
faculty of memory that is so important for autobiography but
so unimportant for biography:

        When Paul and Peter wake up in the same bed,
     and recognize that they have been asleep, each one
     of them mentally reaches back and makes connection
     with but one of the two streams of thought which
     were broken by the sleeping hours.... Peter's
     present instantly finds out Peter's past, and never
     by mistake knits itself on to that of Paul. Paul's
     thought in turn is as little liable to go astray.
     The past thought of Peter is appropriated by the
     present Peter alone. He may have a knowledge, and
     a correct one too, of what Paul's last drowsy states
     of mind were as he sank into sleep, but it is an
     entirely different sort of knowledge from that
     which he has of his own last states. He remembers
     his own states, whilst he only conceives Paul's.
     Remembrance is like direct feeling; its object is
     suffused with a warmth and intimacy to which no
     object of mere conception ever attains. This
     quality of warmth and intimacy and immediacy is
     what Peter's present thought also possesses for
     itself. So sure as this present is me, is mine,
     it says, so sure is anything else that comes with
     the same warmth and intimacy and immediacy, me and
     mine.

Where the autobiographer "remembers," the biographer
"conceives"; and where the former finds the object of his
memory suffused with "warmth and intimacy and immediacy," the
latter must set about discovering a context in which documented events from an alien life will fall into place and take on
a significance that will no doubt be a vastly different
significance from the one memory would give them if this were
his own life and not the life of another man. For memory the
biographer is forced to substitute conceptions - precisely
such conceptions as the life course - to which the life of his
subject may be presumed more or less to conform.

As to the perspective adopted by biographers and autobiographers, Paul Valéry once wrote the following: "I don't
know if anyone has ever tried to write a biography and
attempted at each instant of it to know as little of the
following moment as the hero of the work knew himself at the
corresponding instant of his career. This would be to restore
chance in each instant, rather than putting together a series
that admits of a neat summary and a causality that can be
expressed in a formula." Surely no biographer has ever done
this, though the notion that one might try and the results
that such an attempt would presumably produce are interesting
to comtemplate. If such a biography were ever produced,
however, readers would doubtless rebel, for readers generally
desire a more or less neat summary in their biographies and
they demand that for the events narrated the biographer
discover a causality expressible in such formulae as "mid-
life crisis," "oral/anal personality," "Oedipal fixation,"
"sibling rivalry," etc. These and other formulae are of
course only conceived by an observer who views not only from
after the fact but from outside of it as well. The biographer's perspective, in other words, is nearly always an a
posteriori and external one. The autobiographer's perspective,
too, is a posteriori but it is internal rather than external
and this makes all the difference in the world: when the view
is from within, causality goes out the window and I can think
of no autobiography in which the writer offers a formula for
his life - and precious few that exhibit any kind of neat
summary. On the contrary - and I would say that it is because
of the internal view - autobiography tends to shun summary and
it is most often about as lacking in neatness as any variety
of writing imaginable.

While the typical biography is a highly structured affair,
reflecting the biographer's conception of the structure of the
life course, an autobiography is likely to be largely
unstructured, reflecting the writer's feeling that there has
been no external or generalized pattern that his life has
followed. When an autobiography does display a pattern, it is
almost certain to be teleological, determined by the end

towards which the story moves, i.e., by the writer's present
being. In contrast, when a biography displays a pattern (as
readers feel it must do) it is nearly always causal, looking
for causes in childhood to explain why the man acted as he
did in adulthood. Finalistic vs. deterministic explanations:
thus, the autobiographic vs. biographic understanding.

The pattern of our life is never as clear to us as it is
to others, whether those others be right or wrong. The view
from within is dark and obscure, and what happens to ourselves
often seems a matter of chance; the view from without is
bright and distinct, and what happens to others is not a
matter of chance but of formulaic cause and effect. A
corollary of this fact is that there is a tendency for autobiographies to begin with a relatively clear structural sense
about them but then, as they approach nearer to the present,
to collapse into fragmentariness and uncertainty. It is as
if we can see general childhood in our individual childhood,
but in adulthood we cannot see how like the course of our life
is to the life course. Hence we have formulae to explain the
lives of others but none to explain our own life. In his
Autobiography Charles Darwin records what he calls a "curious
and lamentable loss of the higher aesthetic tastes," but while
he recognizes the loss it nevertheless remains unaccountable
to him, merely curious and puzzling and to a degree
distressing: "I cannot conceive," he says, "what could have
caused the atrophy of that part of the brain alone, on which
the higher tastes depend." Subsequent biographers, on the
other hand, have found it easy to conceive of causes (though
they have not always agreed in their conception since one
biographer's understanding of the life course is not
necessarily the same as another biographer's understanding of
it). Likewise, any biographer adept at "psycho-history" could
produce a formula or a name to account for what John Stuart
Mill in his Autobiography calls "A Crisis in My Mental History,"
but Mill himself hadn't sufficient distance or the necessary
perspective to discover a diagnostic name or an aetiological
formula for his crisis (unless it might have been the name of
his father, James Mill). Going back to Henry Adam's remark,
I doubt that either Darwin or Mill would have been overly
pleased to have his life taken by biographers deducing
aetiologies from the corpse of the once living man.

Another consequence of the opposed perspectives of
biography/autobiography is that while the conclusion of a
biography is frequently the strongest and most moving section
of the book - carrying much of pathos as the course of this
life, now so familiar to the reader, comes to its end - for
most autobiographies there is no conclusion at all, neither in
a literal nor in a rhetorical/structural sense. The auto-

biographer, of course, cannot see the end of his story as the
biographer can do; but there is more to it than this. Who
remembers the end of Mill's Autobiography? Who has ever forgotten its beginning? Or to point the matter more sharply,
everyone remembers the end of The Autobiography of Malcom X
precisely because the conclusion is not a conclusion of the
autobiography but is a biographical epilogue by Alex Haley.
Almost the only way for an autobiographer to escape
fragmentary incconclusiveness is to set clear limits to the
course of life being narrated - Black Boy by Richard Wright,
for example, or L'enfant noir by Camara Laye, or Memories of
a Catholic Girlhood by Mary McCarthy; the same effect of
giving conclusion to a life can be achieved by the fact of
conversion in confessional autobiography - St. Augustine's
Confessions and Bunyan's Grace Abounding to the Chief of
Sinners, for example. Otherwise, without arbitrary limits or
the conclusiveness afforded by conversion, autobiographers
frequently find themselves incapable of completing their
project even to the present - or if not incapable then
uninterested and unwilling. Franklin's Autobiography is a
good case in point: Franklin never finished what he set out
to do, but few readers, I imagine, are disappointed, for his
book simply peters out and the last half is nothing like as
interesting as the first half. Likewise, the last two-thirds
of Rousseau's Confessions, with its endless paranoid confusion,
is plain boring, but the first third, looking back to distant
childhood, provides more than sufficient reason for the book's
classic status. It seems unnecessary to mention contrary
instances in biography for there is no good biography that I
can think of that is not as powerful at the end as throughout
and very frequently biography is more powerful at the end
than elsewhere.

Biographers, as I have implied earlier, often adopt a
"scientific" attitude towards the life course, i.e., they
understand a generalized pattern to which a particular life
more or less conforms, passing through the same stages, in
effect the same course, as other individual lives. The autobiographer, again as I have already suggested, seldom understands what he naturally takes to be his own particular,
unique life in this general way. As an instance of the
"scientific" tendency, numerous biographers of recent times
have had recourse to the science of psychoanalysis to
discern patterns of cause and effect that would otherwise go
unnoticed and uncomprehended. Thus Leon Edel might be said
to adopt a Freudian explanatory model in his rendering of
Henry James's life - or in his taking of James's life. But
in A Small Boy and Others and in Notes of a Son and Brother
James offers us no such pre-cut, scientific, generalized
pattern for his own life. As it were overwhelmed by memories,

real, vivid, and immediately present to him, James suggests
no psychic causality, no model for his own development or
behavior, no pattern of which his life might be supposed an
example. To put it simply, Edel views causally, while James,
observing a consciousness - his present consciousness -
coming into being, views teleologically.

Given the frequency of Freudian biographies, what is
perhaps a more striking instance of this same phenomenon is
that the presumed master of such biographers, i.e., Freud
himself, while thoroughly "Freudian" in his psycho-biographical
study of Leonardo da Vinci, is not particularly so in his own
Autobiographical Study. The pattern discovered by Freud in
Leonardo's life is causal but in his own life is teleogical:
the father of psychoanalysis comes ineluctably into existence
in the Autobiographical Study but the progress is impelled
by a pull from the end, from the present, rather than a push
from the beginning, from the distant past; and Freud offers
no cause/effect explanation for his becoming the father of
psychoanalysis though he can and does offer a cause/effect
explanation of why Leonardo painted certain of his works
just as he did. This, I say, is striking yet not, if one
gives it some thought, illogical: the patterns so clear in
someone else's life - Henry James or Leonardo or the most
recent neurotic patient on the couch - are nothing like so
clear in one's own life, lived as it were not across the
street from the forest but right amid the trees; and I dare
say the life course is more often and more clearly seen by
all of us in other lives than it is in our own. What we see
in ourselves is life; what we see in another is the course of
a life; what we see in generalized others is the life course.
And ringing the changes on these three is the same as moving
from art to science, from autobiography to biography to
sociology and psychology.

Toni Antonucci, Lois M. Tamir,
Steven Dubnoff

3. Mental Health Across the Family Life Cycle

Introduction

The purpose of this research was to explore mental
health as it relates to the family life cycle. In pursuing
this investigation we have made two assumptions: first, that
mental health is a multidimensional rather than a unidimensional phenomenon; and second, that family life stage variation is an important contributing factor to the life experience of an individual.

The use of multidimensional criteria of mental health is
not new, however it has not been universally accepted. Some
have chosen to adopt a unidimensional approach which focuses
on only one particular aspect of mental health, such as
defenses, coping styles or distress, and assume that to be
the criterion of mental health. The assumption that mental
health is unidimensional in many ways simplifies the issue,
since one can assess an individual on a particular dimension
and accept this as an accurate assessment of the individual's
mental health. It is assumed that any one particular measure
does not reveal an individual's overall mental health status
but rather that several measures provide information on a
variety of factors which contribute to overall mental health.
People can therefore be identified as more or less healthy
in a particular sphere depending upon the criterion or area
of functioning in question. In addition, within each area
different questions are used to identify different people as
those who experience trouble, have particular problems or who
feel they are coping well. Thus, we have assumed that psychosocial functioning can only be evaluated with multiple
criteria. For example, adequacy of coping would and should

37

be judged differently in the context of people's evaluation
of their own happiness, in their reports of symptoms, and in
their discussion of informal social supports. There may be
some generality in styles across these areas but it is not
likely to be strong enough to justify adopting a single criterion of mental health.

    We have also adopted a life course perspective, which
emphasizes the importance of examining the developing individual within the context of his or her entire life history,
and extended it to include what we have labelled the family
life cycle. The family life cycle presupposes the importance
of an individual's life situation to his or her individual
mental health. In addition, it assumes that the major problems or issues associated with mental health will change in
parallel with family life cycle development. Although this
approach is not altogether new (Hill, 1968), it is reasonable
to say that it is not well developed, or widely used. However, Campbell, Converse and Rodgers (1976) in their study
on Quality of Life did find that information about the family
life cycle stage was useful in discriminating, for example,
between marital satisfaction and perception of the marital
relationship.

    In the present investigation we have included a seven
level family life stage variable ranging from single adults
to married adults whose children are all over seventeen.
This family life stage is, of course, confounded with age of
respondent but is nevertheless informative. We have also
included ten variables which reflect subjective mental
health. These include measures of overall well being, psychological and physical symptoms, and perceptions of informal
social support. We hypothesized that the combination of the
family life cycle variable and multiple indicators of mental
health would reveal those variations in mental health that
are related to family life stage. This information, in turn,
enabled us to develop profiles highlighting the pertinent
issues for mental health at each of the family life stages.

Method

The Sample

    The two data sets upon which this paper is based are
derived from studies conducted by the Survey Research Center
at The University of Michigan in 1957 (Gurin, Veroff, and Feld,
1960) and 1976 (Douvan, Veroff and Kulka). Both are national
representative sample of over 2000 adults (N=4724), designed
to explore the self-reported mental health of Americans and

the general adjustment they make to the roles they occupy as
parent, spouse, and worker. The national samples included
adults 21 and over living in households in the coterminous
United States, selected by probability sampling procedures.
The interviews were introduced as a study of modern living
and averaged one to one and a half hours in length. The
interview schedule included both open and close ended questions. The open ended questions were coded in the same
manner over the two sample years, thus permitting comparisons
between the two.

Two major cautions in interpreting straight overall comparisons of the 1957 and 1976 data should be emphasized.
First, the 72% response rate to the survey in 1976 was lower
than the 81% achieved in 1957. Unfortunately, all current
large scale surveys have had to contend with this problem.
We may not be reaching some critical groups in the country,
although the major demographic distributions in the 1976
sample was compared with the 1970 census and the 1976 Current
Population Survey and no substantial deviations were found.
Secondly, some obvious demographic shifts within the population have occurred: the 1976 population is more educated,
and has a greater proportion of very young and very old
adults. People are staying single longer and having children
later. Overall sample differences in responses could thus be
attributable to these age or education changes. These are
sources of bias that should be noted.

The family life cycle variable was constructed to represent the course of normal family development. The variable
is divided into seven stages: young singles, young childless
married couples (pre-parents), parents with pre-school children, parents with grade school children, parents with high
school and grade school children (parents of adolescents),
parents of grade school children and children over seventeen
(launching parents) and finally, parents with children all
over seventeen (post-parents). In order to make this variable as representative as possible, singles over thirty-four
have been excluded, as have older married people with no
children (again over 34), divorced people with no children,
divorced or remarried people who either do not see much of
their children or on whom there is too little data to make a
determination, and widows/widowers. Although these exclu-
sions are in part arbitrary, it was felt that these groups
would substantially detract from the modal representative-
ness of the family life cycle variable and/or, as was the
case in several instances, the number of people in these
categories were too few to warrant analysis.

Table 1.   Percentage of Respondents Reporting Feelings of
Happiness over the Family Life Cycle

| Family Life Cycle | Year | How Happy? | | | N |
		Very	Pretty	Not Too	
Males					
Single	1957	9	86	5	44
	1976	24	64	12	89
Childless	1957	36	60	4	47
	1976	39	56	5	59
Any Pre-School	1957	35	59	6	283
	1976	29	63	8	161
Only Grade School	1957	41	54	5	98
	1976	34	61	4	70
High/Grade Schools	1957	34	58	8	88
	1976	22	68	10	63
>17 + Grade School	1957	30	53	17	102
	1976	39	55	6	107
All >17	1957	36	54	9	222
	1976	35	53	12	223
Females					
Single	1957	36	54	11	28
	1976	28	56	16	88
Childless	1957	59	39	2	59
	1976	41	52	7	83
Any Pre-School	1957	44	50	5	318
	1976	36	55	9	193
Only Grade School	1957	46	48	6	127
	1976	41	53	6	113
High/Grade Schools	1957	44	48	8	102
	1976	32	58	9	77
>17 + Grade School	1957	32	57	10	105
	1976	33	55	12	137
All >17	1957	33	51	16	246
	1976	33	60	8	260

Data Analyses

The results reported in this paper are based on the log linear analysis of contingency tables (Goodman, 1972). In each case, the dependent variable was cross-classified by the family stage variable, year of interview, and sex of respondent and analyzed for the separate effects of each variable and their interactions. Results noted in the text reflect statistically significant effects, as estimated from these log linear analyses.

Income Adequacy Analyses

The family life cycle is relatively well correlated with economic well being. In order to test for the possible spuriousness of family life cycle effects, an income variable was used in the 1976 data as a control. This variable, which is the logarithm of the ratio of the respondents' family income to family needs, was created by using the Bureau of Labor Statistics intermediate budget as adjusted for region, size of community, age of household head and number of people in household. This control was applied to all the dependent variables reported below except for such polytomies as sources of informal social support. The effect of the family life cycle was significant in regression analyses controlling for this income variable for most of the non-polytomous variables considered here.

Results

Turning now to the results, we begin with three measures of overall well being: happiness, worries, and self acceptance; then consider three symptoms of distress which have been labelled: psychological anxiety, immobilization, and physical health; and finally, the different strategies people report using to handle worries and unhappiness will be presented.

General Well Being

Exploration of well being through the family life cycle was begun by examining the adult's subjective experience of happiness. Respondents were asked the following question:

Taking all things together, how would you say things are these days--would you say you're very happy, pretty happy, or not too happy?

The effects of the family life cycle on reponses to this question appear in Table 1. Single people are significantly less happy than married people, and childless married persons are generally happier than married people with children.

Table 2. Percentage of Respondents Reporting Frequency of Worrying Over The Family Life Cycle

Family Life Cycle	Year	Always	A Lot	Sometimes	Not Much	Never	N
					Frequency of Worrying		
Males							
Single	1957	2	24	12	44	17	41
	1976	0	42	8	48	2	86
Childless	1957	2	20	11	54	11	44
	1976	2	33	13	47	6	55
Any Pre-School	1957	2	27	10	51	9	280
	1976	6	44	12	35	3	157
Only Grade School	1957	2	28	10	47	14	94
	1976	2	32	7	52	7	68
High/Grade Schools	1957	0	23	10	55	12	82
	1976	2	54	13	29	3	63
>17 + Grade School	1957	1	25	5	60	9	93
	1976	5	28	7	54	7	102
All >17	1957	3	25	3	52	18	211
	1976	2	30	8	50	10	217

Table 2. (continued)

Family Life Cycle	Year	Frequency of Worrying					N
		Always	A Lot	Sometimes	Not Much	Never	
Females							
Single	1957	0	39	4	54	4	28
	1976	1	54	7	36	1	83
Childless	1957	4	29	4	53	11	55
	1976	2	43	12	41	1	81
Any Pre-School	1957	5	33	7	50	4	309
	1976	2	56	7	33	2	186
Only Grade School	1957	8	26	12	48	6	119
	1976	6	53	9	30	3	110
High/Grade Schools	1957	8	29	11	44	7	97
	1976	3	49	5	41	3	74
>17 + Grade School	1957	10	34	12	37	6	99
	1976	3	56	5	35	2	130
All >17	1957	7	33	6	44	10	235
	1976	6	39	9	40	6	244

Parents of grade schoolers are happier than parents of preschoolers, and, in the later stages of the family life cycle,
there is a general decline in happiness.

There were some changes over the two survey years. Only
9% of the single males in 1957 were very happy compared to
23% in 1976. Childless married females in 1957 were more
likely to respond that they were happy than in 1976. Thus,
there seems to have been some important changes for young
people, both singles and young-marrieds, over the last twenty
years.

A very different picture emerges when we examine the
effect of life cycle on worries which is displayed in Table
2. Respondents were first asked: "Everybody has some things
he worries about more or less. What kind of things do you
worry about most?" Following this question, they were then
asked: "Do you worry about such things a lot or not very
much?" The answer to this open-ended question was coded on
a five point scale from "all the time" to "never" and this
constitutes our measure of amount of worrying.

Single people tended to worry "a lot" relative to respondents in the other family life stages. The effect was
most pronounced for males in 1976. Single males tended to
report that they worried "a lot" much more frequently in
1976 than in 1957 (24% vs. 42%) as did fathers of high
schoolers and grade schoolers (23% vs. 54%). Worries were
low for parents of pre-schoolers and respondents whose children were all older than 17. Overall, females report worrying
more than males and this effect is more pronounced in 1976
than in 1957.

A measure of the respondents' willingness to admit their
own shortcomings was tapped with a question about whether
they would like a hypothetical or actual child of the same
sex as themselves to be different from themselves. Following
the statement, "Many people when they think about their children, would like them to be different from themselves in some
ways," respondents were asked how they would like their child
to differ from themselves. If the respondent mentioned a
difference, this variable was scored positively and taken as
a measure of the respondent's willingness to admit his or her
shortcomings. Results appear in Table 3. The family life
cycle has a significant effect on this variable, but this
effect was concentrated in the latest family life cycle
stage, that is, people with children all older than 17.
These, generally older, respondents were considerably less
likely to respond that they wanted their children to differ

Table 3.   Percentage of Respondents Who Admit Shortcomings
           Over the Family Life Cycle

Family Life Cycle	Year	Admit Shortcomings	N
Males			
Single	1957	85	41
	1976	77	90
Childless	1957	80	46
	1976	82	57
Any Pre-School	1957	89	273
	1976	75	157
Only Grade School	1957	86	97
	1976	74	65
High/Grade Schools	1957	88	83
	1976	82	68
>17 + Grade School	1957	79	94
	1976	82	103
All > 17	1957	69	218
	1976	59	209
Females			
Single	1957	93	27
	1976	84	85
Childless	1957	88	59
	1976	88	77
Any Pre-School	1957	88	305
	1976	84	182
Only Grade School	1957	88	113
	1976	86	103
High/Grade Schools	1957	85	100
	1976	86	72
>17 + Grade School	1957	82	101
	1976	79	128
All > 17	1957	67	241
	1976	56	243

Table 4. Psychological and Physical Symptom Items Asked in
          1957 and 1976

Anxiety: Sum of the following five: (These five questions
all have a range of possible answers including (1) nearly
all the time; (2) pretty often; (3) not very much; and (4)
never.)
    (a) "Do you ever have any trouble getting to sleep or
         staying asleep?"
    (b) "Have you ever been bothered by nervousness,
         feeling fidgety and tense?"
    (c) "Are you ever troubled by headaches or pains in
         the head?"
    (d) "Do you have loss of appetite?"
    (e) "How often are you bothered by having an upset
         stomach?"
Immobilization: Sum of the following: (These two questions
also have a range of possible answers including (1) nearly
all the time; (2) pretty often; (3) not very much; and (4)
never.)
    (a) "Do you find it difficult to get up in the morn-
         ing?"
    (b) "Have you ever been bothered by your hands sweat-
         ing so that they are damp and clammy?"
Physical Ill Health: Sum of the following: (The first
three questions had a range of possible answers including
(1) many times; (2) sometimes; (3) hardly ever; and (4)
never.)
    (a) "Has any ill health affected the amount of work
         you do?"
    (b) "Have you ever been bothered by shortness of
         breath when you were not exercising or working
         hard?"
    (c) "Have you ever been bothered by your heart beating
         hard?"
    (d) "Here are some more questions like those you've
         filled out. This time just answer 'yes' or 'no.'
         Do you feel you are bothered by all sorts of pains
         and ailments in different parts of your body?"
         (1) yes, (2) no, weighted 4,2 respectively for the
         scale.
    (e) "For the most part, do you feel healthy enough to
         carry out the things that you would like to do?"
         (1) yes, (2) no, weighted 2,4 respectively for the
         scale.
    (f) "Do you have any particular physical or health
         trouble?" (1) yes, (2) no, weighted 4,2 respec-
         tively for the scale.

---

from themselves. Males were, in general, less likely to
admit their shortcomings than females.

Symptoms

Numerous questions concerning physical and emotional
symptoms were asked of respondents in 1957 and 1976. Factor
analyses were then conducted by Veroff, Douvan, and Kulka
(forthcoming) yielding three general symptoms factors. These
were labelled: psychological anxiety, immobilization, and
physical ill health (see Table 4 for specific questions).
Each factor was examined separately. Results appear in
Table 5.

Psychological anxiety includes symptoms such as insom-
nia, nervousness and headaches. This variable is considered
a useful indicator of psychological well being. Although
five levels of psychological anxiety, ranging from low to
high were analyzed, only the highest level of anxiety is of
theoretical and practical importance. At any of the other
levels, symptoms remain relatively infrequent. With the
highest level we have confidence that we are dealing with
reports of moderate to high levels of symptoms.

The family life stage variable reveals that the highest
level of psychological anxiety occurs within the middle life
stage groups where respondents are parents of grade schoolers
and/or high schoolers, or parents of children both above and
below age 17. This trend is more prominent within families
where high schoolers and children over 17 along with grade
schoolers are present, and less so when only grade schoolers
are in the home. It is important to note, however, that it
is primarily the females within these stages who are exhibiting the comparatively higher incidences of psychological
anxiety symptoms. Approximately 25% of the women in these
groups manifest these symptoms at high levels. This finding,
which is curvilinear, since it is concentrated around those
stages in the middle of the life cycle, may be indicative of
the transitional nature of this life stage, where the woman

Table 5. Percentage of Respondents Reporting "High" Symptoms Over the Family Life Cycle

| Family Life Cycle | Year | Symptoms | | | |
		Psychological Anxiety	Immobilization	Physical Health Problems	N
Males					
Single	1957	4	52	2	44
	1976	9	29	3	92
Childless	1957	2	23	0	47
	1976	12	26	3	61
Any Pre-School	1957	9	25	4	284
	1976	12	24	3	161
Only Grade School	1957	9	21	5	98
	1976	10	24	6	71
High/Grade Schools	1957	9	16	8	88
	1976	10	11	8	71
>17 + Grade School	1957	16	22	15	101
	1976	16	21	11	107
All >17	1957	9	12	17	225
	1976	11	8	23	219

Table 5. (continued)

		Symptoms			
Family Life Cycle	Year	Psychological Anxiety	Immobilization	Physical Health Problems	N
Females					
Single	1957	4	29	4	28
	1976	18	26	1	88
Childless	1957	8	19	10	59
	1976	16	37	4	82
Any Pre-School	1957	15	41	9	320
	1976	19	25	5	193
Only Grade School	1957	14	39	7	127
	1976	26	22	8	113
High/Grade Schools	1957	29	30	11	101
	1976	25	26	8	77
>17 + Grade School	1957	23	21	19	105
	1976	26	25	20	135
All >17	1957	24	15	25	247
	1976	19	16	23	264

is no longer responsible for extensive daily care of her youngest child, and must develop new routines of behavior. Additionally, the individual must adjust to the presence of an adolescent in the home. An overall year difference in incidence of reporting high psychological anxiety is also evident. In general more people in 1976 than in 1957 are willing to report psychological anxiety.

The factor of immobilization includes the symptoms of difficulties rising in the morning and sweating hands. It has been suggested (Veroff and Depner, 1978) that this variable assesses the respondent's difficulties in decision-making. Four levels of immobilization are found, but again only the highest level is reported.

In general, females are more likely than males to report high levels of immobilization symptoms. The family stage variable indicates, however, that the highest overall frequencies of immobilization occur among single adults and parents of preschoolers. Single adults exhibiting high levels of immobilization may be lacking the support systems necessary for efficient action. And parents of preschoolers may be immobilized by the onslaught of responsibilities which accompany the care of a young child. It is also important to note that the life stage group where children are already grown (that is, over 17) reports high levels of immobiliza-tion least frequently. These adults are more likely to have settled into life styles with which they are comfortable, that is, they have decreased responsibilities and pressures and have more time to dedicate to their own pursuits.

Interestingly, a family stage by year interaction indi-cates higher levels of immobilization among single adults in 1957 and 1976, and higher levels of immobilization among childless adults in 1976 and 1957. Within the singles group, this interaction may be accounted for primarily by the males, who drop from 52% to 29% reporting high levels of immobiliza-tion. This finding is most likely a function of the greater acceptance of single life styles in 1976 than 1957. Within the childless group, the interaction may be accounted for primarily by the females, who increase from 19% to 37% re-porting high levels of immobilization. This finding may be due to the intensified conflict at this stage concerning the decision to have children and/or pursue career goals outside the home.

Our measure of physical ill health reflects distress about the body (Veroff and Depner, 1978). Again, there are five levels of physical ill health but we report only the highest level. The family stage variable indicates that

members of the earlier life stages, especially single adults
and parents of preschoolers report high levels of ill health
far less frequently than people of the later stages, especially parents of children over 17 (who comprise the oldest
age group). Of course, this finding is confounded by the
fact that age increases with family life stage and physical
health often decreases, while concern about health increases
with age.

Handling Worries and Unhappiness

In order to examine what people do when they are faced
with problems, we asked about how people handle worries and
unhappiness. Turning first to the question of worries, we
asked, "If something is on your mind that is bothering you or
worrying you and you do not know what to do about it, what do
you usually do?" If the person mentioned talking it over
with someone, the interviewer asked or noted with whom; if
the person did not mention talking it over with someone, the
interviewer probed: "Do you ever talk it over with anyone?
Who is that?" Responses to this question were coded into
seven categories: (1) passive reactions, which included dis-
placement or denial, doing nothing, continuing tension; (2)
prayer, which included actually praying, turning to the
scriptures or mention of trusting in the Lord; (3) doing
something, if an individual actually mentioned taking some
immediate action to cope with the situation; (4) informal
social support, coded if the respondent mentioned talking it
over with informal sources such as family, friends, neigh-
bors; (5) formal support, coded if the individual mentioned
a more formal source, such as lawyer, doctor, clergy, psychi-
atrist, etc. An exactly parallel question was asked about
how people handle unhappiness with similarly parallel coding.
With regard to talking unhappiness over with someone, however, this question was coded in a fashion identical to that
in the question regarding worries but only if the person
volunteered that s/he talked unhappiness over with someone.
Talking over unhappiness was not specifically probed. This
may account for the parallel but somewhat reduced proportions
of people reporting talking over unhappiness with others.

Family stage comparisons of how people handle worries
and unhappiness appear in Tables 6 and 7. Differences in
three categories, prayer, coping and informal social support,
emerge. Singles and childless couples generally pray less,
but people with children in grade school or older (that is,
with children in high school or over 17) report praying more.
These differences are, of course, again confounded with age
since older people generally report praying more than younger
people. With regard to coping, singles report more coping in

Table 6. Percentage of Respondents Reporting How They Handle Worries Over the Family Life Cycle

		Handles Worries					
Family Life Cycle	Year	Passive	Prayer	Coping	Informal Help	N
Males						
Single	1957	41	0	25	23	44
	1976	29	4	24	36	92
Childless	1957	19	0	30	36	47
	1976	21	3	31	41	61
Any Pre-School	1957	33	6	21	31	284
	1976	25	3	27	40	162
Only Grade School	1957	31	4	22	32	98
	1976	28	13	18	35	71
High/Grade Schools	1957	40	6	25	19	88
	1976	28	10	30	31	71
>17 + Grade School	1957	43	12	24	10	102
	1976	34	13	20	22	108
All >17	1957	45	12	16	14	225
	1976	34	11	18	25	225

Table 6. (continued)

| Family Life Cycle | Year | Handles Worries | | | | |
		Passive	Prayer	Coping	Informal Help	N
Females						
Single	1957	18	7	29	39	28
	1976	17	8	19	49	88
Childless	1957	20	15	8	52	59
	1976	14	5	11	68	83
Any Pre-School	1957	30	11	8	41	320
	1976	16	7	9	60	194
Only Grade School	1957	30	16	13	37	127
	1976	26	10	11	38	113
High/Grade Schools	1957	31	17	12	33	102
	1976	24	14	10	45	78
>17 + Grade School	1957	26	33	10	23	105
	1976	23	20	19	34	137
All >17	1957	33	32	7	20	247
	1976	27	24	14	26	265

Table 7. Percentage of Respondents Reporting How They Handle Unhappiness Over the Family Life Cycle

| Family Life Cycle | Year | Handles Unhappiness | | | | N |
		Passive	Prayer	Coping	Informal Help	
Males						
Single	1957	25	11	14	27	44
	1976	37	9	15	20	92
Childless	1957	28	17	11	26	47
	1976	25	7	15	28	61
Any Pre-School	1957	29	19	7	13	284
	1976	13	15	13	33	162
Only Grade School	1957	24	25	13	15	98
	1976	20	24	13	30	71
High/Grade Schools	1957	30	17	8	19	88
	1976	28	22	7	27	71
>17 + Grade School	1957	22	30	7	13	102
	1976	19	25	14	26	108
All >17	1957	23	27	11	17	225
	1976	30	17	7	22	225

Table 7. (continued)

Family Life Cycle	Year	Handles Unhappiness				
		Passive	Prayer	Coping	Informal Help	N
Females						
Single	1957	21	32	4	29	28
	1976	17	11	3	47	88
Childless	1957	20	36	5	20	59
	1976	28	5	11	35	83
Any Pre-School	1957	22	33	3	27	320
	1976	20	20	7	36	194
Only Grade School	1957	20	32	6	26	127
	1976	15	24	4	37	113
High/Grade Schools	1957	22	38	3	16	102
	1976	22	24	5	31	78
>17 + Grade School	1957	18	47	2	18	105
	1976	19	34	7	26	105
All >17	1957	19	45	8	17	247
	1976	19	35	3	30	265

response to worries than other groups, and people with children over 17 report less coping. No family life stage differences in coping are indicated for unhappiness. In the case of informal social supports, however, the results for worries and unhappiness are again parallel. In general people in the younger family life stages (childless people and those with preschoolers) report higher use of informal social support than people in the two later family life stages (that is, people with grade school children or older). This effect is true for both worries and unhappiness but may also be confounded by age. Younger people may have more people to talk with than older people, or older people may simply be more internally oriented.

Our results also indicate that there are overall year and sex differences. To summarize very briefly, people report being less passive in 1976 than in 1957. The sex differences indicate that men are more passive than women, that women pray more than men, and that generally men report more coping responses but women report much more use of informal social support than men. These results are similar for both worries and unhappiness.

As mentioned earlier, we also asked people with whom they talked with when worried and unhappy. Results appear in Tables 8 and 9. People with preschool children report talking to friends when worried and unhappy less than people in other family life stages especially the earlier ones. In addition, childless males generally report sharing their worries with friends comparatively less. Also of interest is the consistent trend that married women in 1976, regardless of life stage, report sharing their worries with spouse exclusively much less than married women in 1957 or married men in either year.

Discussion

Family Life Stage Profiles

Each stage of the family life cycle represents a unique constellation of social and psychological conditions. In turn, the mental health of individuals at each of these stages is effected in unique ways. The environment, family structure, and age of the individual work jointly to shape the well being of the developing adult. The present section, based upon the preceding analyses, outlines modal profiles of the conditions of well being across the family life cycle.

Single adults remain comparatively less happy than adults who are married. They worry more and are more immo-

bilized than adults at other life stages. Since the adults
aged 21-35 are expected to marry, perhaps this group of young
adults finds themselves in the tedious position of having to
explain their singlehood. Yet, young, single adults appear
to be quite resilient. They display relatively higher frequencies of coping mechanisms in response to those concerns
they worry about. And males in particular describe themselves as more happy and less immobilized in 1976 as compared
with 20 years previously. This finding appears to indicate
that the social environment is becoming more tolerant of and
accommodating to the single life style.

   Married childless adults, in contrast, report greater
happiness than those with children. They make extensive use
of informal social networks to deal with worries and
unhappiness, yet the men tend to utilize friends in this
manner less frequently. This group, therefore, appears to
display a high degree of integration within family and community networks, as well as the luxury of an available spouse
with whom to confide. Paradoxically, young married and
childless females have increased in reported happiness from
1957 to 1976, yet have also increased in reported immobilization symptoms. Perhaps these women have become enthused by
the broadened opportunities available to them within the current generation, but become immobilized when confronted with
these multiple options among which they must choose: career,
motherhood, or the difficult combination of both.

   Parents of preschool children continue the pattern of
high usage of informal support networks yet they make less
use of friends to talk over worries and unhappiness. Perhaps the immense burden of caring for a young child or children limits these adults' opportunities for newly establishing and maintaining friendship links, especially with others
who are not under similar parenting constraints. Parents of
preschoolers also report less happiness than adults whose
children are already in grade school, and high degrees of
immobilization. They worry less, however. This is most
likely because they are more concerned with the day to day
details of caring for a small child than with worrisome long
range goals.

   Parents of gradeschoolers display no outstanding mental
health traits of either a positive or negative nature for the
variables we have examined. The key to this stage, therefore, is moderation. Goals are set; routines are solidified;
and happiness, symptom reports, and support networks are unex-
treme. Life cycle research to date supports this conclusion.
Males at this stage of their lives typically dedicate themselves to their career goals, with less internal reflection

Table 8. Percentage of Respondents Reporting Sources of Help When Worried Over the Family Life Cycle

			Source of Help When Worried			
Family Life Cycle	Year	Spouse Exclusively	Multiple Family Members	Friends	Other	N
Males						
Single	1957	0	55	18	27	11
	1976	0	20	74	6	35
Childless	1957	65	20	0	15	20
	1976	65	23	4	8	26
Any Pre-School	1957	67	9	8	17	102
	1976	71	14	4	10	69
Only Grade School	1957	65	8	8	19	37
	1976	88	8	4	0	25
High/Grade Schools	1957	74	0	16	10	19
	1976	50	4	41	4	22
>17 + Grade School	1957	69	0	0	31	13
	1976	65	4	12	19	26
All >17	1957	57	7	4	32	44
	1976	62	5	21	13	63

Table 8. (continued)

Family Life Cycle	Year	Spouse Exclusively	Multiple Family Members	Friends	Other	N
Females						
Single	1957	0	46	38	15	13
	1976	0	29	57	14	49
Childless	1957	69	16	12	3	32
	1976	44	21	33	2	57
Any Pre-School	1957	64	16	10	11	147
	1976	49	28	14	10	126
Only Grade School	1957	70	16	8	6	50
	1976	47	14	33	7	58
High/Grade Schools	1957	69	14	11	6	36
	1976	37	26	29	8	38
>17 + Grade School	1957	48	30	11	11	27
	1976	47	31	16	6	49
All >17	1957	60	20	9	11	55
	1976	43	22	16	18	81

Source of Help When Worried

Table 9. Percentage of Respondents Reporting Sources of Help When Unhappy Over the Family Life Cycle

		Source of Help When Unhappy				
Family Life Cycle	Year	Spouse Exclusively	Multiple Family Members	Friends	Other	N
Males						
Single	1957	0	31	44	25	16
	1976	0	23	46	31	26
Childless	1957	12	31	31	25	16
	1976	5	35	28	33	43
Any Pre-School	1957	20	26	28	25	83
	1976	14	48	20	18	65
Only Grade School	1957	16	26	37	21	19
	1976	20	40	24	16	25
High/Grade Schools	1957	15	20	50	15	20
	1976	32	41	14	14	22
>17 + Grade School	1957	39	17	17	28	18
	1976	21	45	31	3	29
All >17	1957	29	22	31	18	45
	1976	19	32	21	28	68

Table 9. (continued)

| Family Life Cycle | Year | Source of Help When Unhappy | | | | |
		Spouse Exclusively	Multiple Family Members	Friends	Other	N
Females						
Single	1957	0	46	27	27	11
	1976	0	32	45	23	53
Childless	1957	12	24	35	29	17
	1976	5	35	28	33	43
Any Pre-School	1957	22	34	22	22	107
	1976	14	41	26	19	85
Only Grade School	1957	12	37	28	23	43
	1976	20	29	33	18	51
High/Grade Schools	1957	9	32	27	32	22
	1976	3	43	33	20	30
>17 + Grade School	1957	12	27	35	27	26
	1976	15	35	26	24	46
All >17	1957	17	40	27	17	48
	1976	22	33	33	12	89

than arises at later stages (Levinson, 1978). Women at this
life stage have often developed their household routines, be
it one which is dedicated to household engineering and, for
example, community service, or one which combines work and
parenting responsibilities within a predictable daily
schedule.

Parents of children who are in grade school and in high
school begin a decline in happiness which continues through
the remaining stages. This appears to be an age-linked finding. It is consonant with other survey research which shows
a decline in happiness with increasing age but a concomitant
increase in life satisfaction (Campbell et al., 1976). The
exuberance of the early life stages, where the future holds
great prospects, is replaced by a more subdued satisfaction
with the life one has lived and one's current security. Yet
parents of high school and grade school children display high
levels of psychological anxiety. Men in particular report
that they worry a great deal. Perhaps this is a function of
the initial presence of an adolescent in the home. The adolescent child has the capacity to rekindle the parents own,
earlier, adolescent conflicts. And the family must cope with
the further strain of contending with a member who now de-
sires to be independent of their authority.

Parents of gradeschoolers and children over 17 years,
hence, similarly display high levels of psychological anxiety, particularly the women. This is most likely linked to
the unsettled and transitional nature of the family during
this stage. The woman, especially if she has dedicated herself to childcare responsibilities until this point, must now
find new activities to occupy her time, as children are gradually launched from the home.

The final family stage consists of adults whose children
are all over 17 years of age. These adults have less worries,
are less immobilized and are less likely to admit shortcomings
in terms of wishing that their offspring were different from
themselves. In spite of increased ill health, presumably due
to advancing age, this stage of adulthood appears more tem-
pered and less conflictful than earlier life stages. The
future has become fairly well delineated, and the marital
couple now has the time for settling into a life style which
they can accommodate solely to their own needs. The burdens
of rearing their children have been lifted. They can now
come to terms with themselves.

Conclusions

The family life cycle variable and the use of multiple
indicators of mental health have provided a rich and varied

assessment of mental health in a select portion of two national populations over 20 years. The findings reported
above suggest not only that the family life course has an
important influence on various aspects of mental health but
also that the inter-relationships among the multiple indicators are not constant over different family life stages.
These findings provide additional insight into the more
general and difficult problem of understanding mental health.
Future research should include the family life cycle as a
significant contributing and possibly mediating factor in the
overall mental health of an individual. The present findings
suggest that it is important to explore feelings of well
being, reported psychological and physical symptoms, and
methods of handling worries and unhappiness with an awareness
of the similarities between any particular individual and
other people in his or her parallel family life cycle stage.
Additional research should also explore the patterns and
inter-relationships among mental health indicators of those
individuals who were excluded from the present study, that
is, people who do not conform to the "normal" or more traditional family life cycle, to examine the similarities and
differences in mental health these people exhibit in comparison with their more traditional counterparts. In sum, both
the family life cycle variable and the use of multiple indicators of mental health provide important information concerning overall mental health in a select "normal" sample
drawn from a national representative sample of the United
States. These findings are useful both in application to
mental health issues in the general population and in exploring mental health issues in more unusual or nontraditional
populations.

References

Campbell, A., Converse, P., & Rodgers, W. 1976. The quality of life. New York: Russel Sage Foundation.

Douvan, E., Veroff, J., & Kulka, R. 1976. A study of modern living. Institute for Social Research, The University of Michigan.

Goodman, L.A. 1972. A general model for the analysis of surveys. American Journal of Sociology, 77, 1035-1086.

Gurin, G., Veroff, J., & Feld, S. 1960. Americans view their mental health. New York: Basic Books.

Hill, R. 1968. Decision making and the family life cycle. In B. L. Neugarten (ed.), Middle age and aging. Chicago: University of Chicago Press.

Levinson, D. J. 1978. The seasons of a man's life. New York: Alfred A. Knopf.

Veroff, J., & Depner, C. November 1978. Changes in perceived well being. Paper presented at the 31st Annual Meeting of the Gerontology Society, Dallas.

Veroff, J., Douvan, E. & Kulka, R. Forthcoming. Americans view their mental health: 1957-1976.

4. A Demographic Approach to the Life Cycle

The past decade has seen a good deal of interdisciplinary social science research on the life course. Psychologists, Sociologists, Historians, Anthropologists, and many others have shared platforms such as this one; read the work of people who come to life course studies with different information, skills and questions; and made use of "foreign" insights in their own work. Demographers have shared in and profited from this interdisciplinary communication. It is tempting here to sing a paean to the pleasure of shared problems and successes. The purpose of this chapter[1], however, is to describe a demographic approach to the life cycle. To accomplish that task, it will be necessary to suppress the celebration of interdisciplinary similarities and stress those ways the disciplines differ in their use of life cycle ideas.

Each discipline uses and understands life cycle facts and ideas in subtly different ways. These differences occur because each discipline understands the life cycle in relation to its own central notions and interests. Thus, facts about the life course have meaning to some psychologists and psychiatrists in relation to the development of intrapsychic structures, to some sociologists in relation to the concept of socialization, and to some anthropologists and historians in relation to the web of a specific culture. It is important to call attention to this notion of meaning-as-relation in discussing a demographic approach to the life cycle because the central idea and its relationship to the life cycle is rather different in demography than in psychology, sociology or anthropology.

---

[1]This research was supported by National Science Foundation Grant #SOC75-20409.

The basic problem in demography is that of population projection. How large will the population be in, say the year 2000? What will be the age distribution in that year? What fraction of the population will be of working age? How many people will be entering college, looking for first jobs, or buying houses? Finding ways of answering these kinds of questions is the raison d'être of demography. The central idea which accomplishes the projection is the population renewal process. This idea is expressed in a number of ways but briefly it is the notion of a cohort of individuals, born in a single year, living out their lives over time subject to a set of age specific fertility and mortality rates. In each year deaths occur to the first generation cohort in accordance with the age specific mortality rates. As the cohort ages through the fertile years, births occur according to the age specific fertility rates. In the year they are born, second-generation children enter the population at age zero and are subsequently subject to growing older and the chances of dying. Because these second generation people are born in accordance to the age specific fertility rates applying to the initial cohort, their births are distributed over time. Thus the children of a single birth cohort are distributed over a number of succeeding birth cohorts.

As the earliest born of the second generation people age into the fertile years, they have children according to an age specific fertility schedule. Because the earliest born second generation cohort will begin to bear children before the initial cohort has aged out of the fertile years, the first crop of third generation babies will share their birth cohort with second generation babies. From that time forward the parents of a single birth cohort will be spread over preceding birth cohorts. As time passes, the initial cohort will disappear through the force of mortality, succeeding generations will have children and eventually the period age distribution will assume a form typical of human populations.

The renewal process as described above will suffice to project the population by age given appropriate assumptions about changing fertility and mortality. The process is easily generalized to project the population by regional location and/or by social characteristics.

Life cycle notions and facts are certainly built into this central idea in demography. In the following pages I want to comment on several implications of the way these notions and facts are related to the demographer's central idea.

The first issue is that life cycle facts are part of the explicans of demographic idea rather than its explicandium. They are a part of the explanation rather than a part of, or derivative from, the thing to be explained which in demography is the future population. Such a relation of life cycle facts to the central disciplinary idea is different from that existing in some other disciplines. A Piagetian psychologist, I imagine, sees life cycle facts as derivative from the intrapsychic cognitive structure, the explication of that structure being the raison d'être of his work. For most structuralists, I suspect, life cycle facts are outcomes rather than inputs to the central process.

The demographer's focus on life cycle facts as inputs to the renewal process has two implications. The first is that those life cycle facts which interest us are the ones which have consequences for the projection process. Thus, demographers have studied changes in the timing of births in the life course because those changes have demographic consequences. Changes in the volume and timing of marriages are studied because they impact births. Many demographers are currently investigating the changing pattern of female labor force participation over the life course because of its impact on marriage and fertility. Through such a retrogression in the causal order, life cycle events become explicandum in demography, but only for the moment, as it were, and only for the sake of the renewal process. Thus, the first implication of life course facts as inputs in demography is that this relation limits and defines those life course facts which are of interest to the demographer.

The second implication refers to the form in which those facts will be cast by demographers. Demographers are widely known to be fussy about their numbers -- to spend a lot of time getting their facts right. Getting the facts right in this context usually means two things. First, it means being sure they represent the whole of the population of interest. That means dealing with distributions as well as central tendencies; being sure that the women who never have children and the women who have fifteen babies are represented as well as the women who have two or three. Getting the numbers right also means expressing them properly in terms of the needs of the renewal process. In general, the renewal process requires that the life cycle facts be expressed as probabilities of transition from one life cycle stage to another. Generating such probabilities requires counting transitions in a year and dividing that count by the life years of exposure to the risk of such an occurrence. Figuring out exposure is a bother because one must determine for each member of the population whether that member is at

risk of the event and for how long. The bother is worth it,
however, because only when life cycle facts are expressed as
a distribution of transition probabilities do they have
demographic meaning, i.e., meaning in relation to the renewal
process.

The life cycle's relation to the population renewal
process as input, then, has two important implications for
what demographers will natively do in studying the life
course. They will pay attention to those aspects of the life
cycle which have demographic consequences and they will cast
the facts about those aspects in terms of a distribution
over age of a sequence of transition probabilities.

A second aspect of the demographers' understanding of
the life cycle has to do with levels of aggregation. The
subject of the renewal process is the population as a whole.
The explanatory disaggregation of this whole is into birth
cohorts. It is to these cohorts that the notion of a life
course is seen to apply by demographers. Certainly the life
course of a cohort is the accumulation of the sequence of
life events occurring to its individual members. Certainly
demographers use and occasionally concoct behavioral theories
to predict those individual sequences. But from among the
potential theories of individual behavior, demographers will
almost unfailingly choose those, usually more primitive,
theories which permit simple aggregation to the cohort in a
fashion which represents the heterogeneity of individual
experience. The demographers' attitude towards the theories
of individual behavior which they use is often distressing
to people from disciplines whose central idea is about or
closely related to individual behavior. The demographer
seems cavalier, even sacrilegious, in a single minded
attention to the predictive power of the theory as opposed to
its adequacy, meaning or even truth in relation to central
ideas in, say psychology, economics, or sociology.

Taken together, these two aspects of the relationship
of the life cycle to the central idea of demography permit a
statement of the demographic view of the life cycle.
Demographers see the life cycle as the collection of transition probabilities between life course stages which have
demographic implications and which pertain to a series of
birth cohorts.

Certainly this is a specialized, even narrow, view of
the life course. It would be silly to propose it as the
only sound understanding of our common subject, for other
disciplines can produce other definitions of the relevant
facts about the life course which are equally meaningful due

to their coherence with other central ideas.

The situation we face is one which has been discussed at some length in recent works in the philosophy of science. It is commonplace in some parts of that field to comment on the theory-ladenness of facts. I take these comments to mean that what a scholar chooses to pay attention to, the way he chooses to represent the facts, and his view of their meaning is intimately connected with his theory. Thus people with different theories may look at the same subject, "see" different things, assemble information about the subject differently, and "understand" quite differently. This circumstance is frustrating to those who believe that the truth about a subject should be unitary. In the social sciences the demand for unitary theory has often led to doctrinal disputes as to whose truth is the best one or to attempts to pool immiscible ideas into a grand but vacuous theory. Some philosophers of science argue that a better course is for each discipline to proceed in working out its own ideas, understandings, and definitions of facts. In this process it sometimes happens that one discipline will produce facts having considerable meaning to a second discipline.

In such a circumstance the webs of meaning of the two disciplines are connected and real progress towards a broader understanding is achieved. Such an occurrence is most productive when the intradisciplinary webs of meaning are relatively coherent. Hence the coherence of the demographic view of the life cycle may, despite its narrowness, provide a relatively powerful engine which can be used in the service of nondemographic interests. Perhaps the interest non-demographers have shown in the cohort idea lends credence to this hope.

In the following pages I will attempt to suggest some ways and provide some examples of how the demographic view of the life cycle may provide notions and facts which are interesting to non-demographers. It will be a chancy attempt because it is hard for an outsider to have a very good "feel" for what will have meaning to insiders in another discipline. Perhaps the best tack is to look at the heart of the renewal process and ask whether there are non-demographic aspects of that center which may be exploited for this purpose.

The heart of the renewal process is the production of one generation by another. Certainly there are other intergenerational relations besides "production." There are strong emotional ties between children and their parents. Parents are widely regarded as important in the guiding of the psychic and cognitive development of their children in

the early years. They are salient socialization agents for
many years. There is important intergenerational trans-
mission of socioeconomic characteristics. There are
important economic ties of dependency; initial dependency of
children on their parents and frequently eventual dependency
of parents on children. Can the demographic view say
anything interesting about these non-demographic inter-
generational relations and the life cycle? I will make two
rather different attempts. The first uses demographic ideas
rather loosely to make a point about secular social trends
and intergenerational differences. The second uses the
machinery of the renewal process more formally to reveal a
changing aspect of the later part of the cohort life cycle
which may have non-demographic meaning.

What things produce generational differences? One
reason the generations are different is because they have
lived through different times. The children of the Great
Depression are different from their parents and from their
own children because of the impact the 1930's had on them.
Second World War veterans had difficulty understanding their
children's attitude towards the Vietnam war. So long as
historical events are regarded as unique there is little the
demographic view can add to our understanding except to
project demographic effects. To the degree that historical
events can be regarded as part of a reasonably orderly
secular trend, however, the demographic view may offer some
insight. Indeed, a major research effort in demography is
currently devoted to understanding the ways long cycles in
economic growth produce generational differences in perception of the disposable income available for having children.
Rather than describe that work, let me take a simpler
example.

It is an old social science notion that many secular
trends roughly follow an S shaped curve. The urbanization
of the American population, the fraction of the population
participating in the industrial economy, the rising educational level of the population are examples. As a sequence
of cohorts are born into a society undergoing such secular
change, they capture and crystalize in their own characteristics the part of the trend they experience. Thus the
proportion of a birth cohort that grew up in an urban
environment or began its working life in the industrial
economy represents the timing of the cohorts life cycle with
respect to the secular trend. Figures for cohorts, then
will reproduce the S shaped secular trend. But what about
generational differences? The length of a generation is
between twenty-five and thirty years, so the difference
between the generations can be estimated as the difference

between points on the S shaped curve which are twenty-five
or thirty years apart. Those differences initially will be
slight. They will increase as the S shaped curve begins to
rise and reach a maximum when change is most rapid. As rise
in the secular trend slows, differences will decrease and
eventually again be slight as the trend reaches its maximum.
Thus an S shaped secular trend produces a trend in generational differences which is like an upside down U. If we
have been going through massive secular change over the past
100 years in urbanization and industrialization and those
changes have been slowing, then relevant generational
differences are likely to be diminishing and our historical
experience about the variables which separate the generations
cause generational conflict, and influence the way parents
and children regard each other is a poor predictor for the
future. If, as seems predicted by the "slowing of growth"
rhetoric, these social trends are not replaced by other
changes having equally massive results, then we may see a
general diminution of generational differences. On the other
hand, if other major secular trends are implied in the
development of post industrial society, then generational
differences will persist but be based on new dimensions which
will have new imports for the participants.

An example of a specific trend which has followed the S
shaped rise is that of educational level. We can see something of the effect of this trend on generational differences
in Figure 1. Plotted in this figure is the proportion of
male respondents in two large national surveys reporting
more education for themselves than for their fathers. The
bottom axis of the figure is the birth year of the cohort.
The surveys were taken in 1962 and 1973. The upper line is
for the later date and its generally higher level is
probably due to differences in the way questions were asked.
The decline for more recently born cohorts is exaggerated
because some young men will complete additional education
after the date of the survey. Nonetheless, the general
concave downwards shape of the graph is evident in both
surveys. The long standing American expectation that sons
will usually have more education than their fathers may be
becoming a thing of the past.

Use of the demographic approach to the life cycle to
investigate the effect of secular trends on generational
differences such as those alluded to above raise questions
well beyond the demographic. How will relations between the
generations be different when most parents and children have
similar levels of formal education? As main features of the
urban, industrial economy settle down, as parents and their
children are born into more similar social worlds, will the

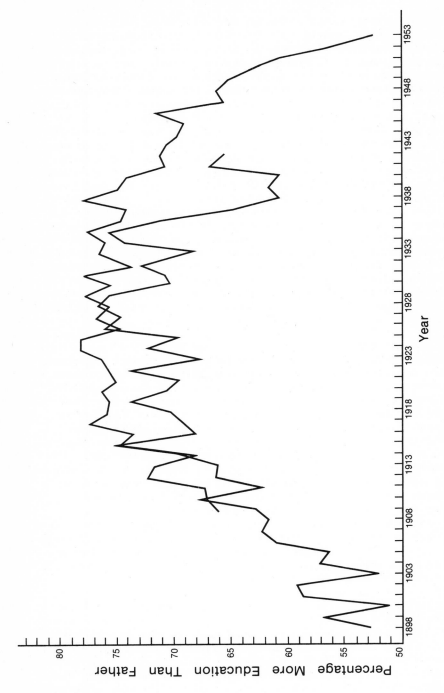

Figure 1.   Percentage of respondents with more education than fathers - ages 20-64.

value of experience increase? Will our view of the elderly
return to that veneration of wisdom traditional of slow-
changing societies? How are the answers to such questions
related to newer secular trends such as the rise in marital
dissolution and the changing nature of the family? These
are questions whose answers require more than demographic
insight.

The above example uses demographic ideas rather loosely,
relying on the mean length of a generation and the expression
of secular trends in cohort characteristics. Can a more
formal exercise of the demographic engine produce life cycle
facts of interest to non-demographers?

A fact of considerable importance in the individual life
course is the death of a parent. Finding ways of using the
demographic machinery to estimate orphanhood is an old demographic topic (1) and the methods for estimating the numbers
of people having surviving kin of various kinds is a topic
of some recent interest (2-4). Perhaps an application of
these methods to data for selected U.S. cohorts will be a
useful example of the demographic approach to the life cycle.

Table 1 presents the percent of living women having
living mothers by age for selected cohorts. Producing these
numbers requires collecting the age distribution of mothers
for each birth cohort and surviving and accumulating them to
various of their children's ages. The age distribution of
mothers is available from vital statistics reports. Cohort
life tables for surviving the mothers are available from
Jacobson (5). Because changes in mortality are rather
orderly, it is possible to complete life tables for cohorts
who are still living by a fairly reliable estimation. The
procedure used presumes that the life changes for mothers is
the same as for all women of the same age in the same birth
cohort.

These figures show that experiencing the death of one's
mother is moving toward older years for more recent cohorts.
Half of living women had a living mother at age 49 for the
1920 birth cohort, while for the 1970 cohort the comparable
age will be about 58.

Elsewhere I have argued that it is useful to hold that
a life cycle transition begins for a cohort when 25 percent
of the members have experienced the event and is completed
when 75 percent have experienced it. For the cohort of 1920,
by this notion, the transition began at about age 35 and ends
at about 59, taking 24 years to complete. For the birth
cohort of 1970 the transition will not begin until about age

Table 1. Estimated Percent of Living Women Having Living
Mothers by Age for Selected U.S. Birth Cohorts

	1970	1960	1950	1930	1920
10	99.2	99.0	98.7	96.5	95.1
20	98.1	97.4	96.6	92.4	89.4
30	95.5	94.3	92.8	85.9	81.2
40	89.4	86.6	84.6	74.4	68.0
50	73.4	67.8	65.3	54.6	47.3
60	41.8	35.9	33.2	27.2	22.2
70	9.5	7.6	6.4	5.4	4.1

	Age at Interpolated Percentiles				
25%	49	47	46	40	35
50%	58	56	55	52	49
75%	64	63	62	61	54
Range	15	16	16	21	24

49 and will be completed by age 64, taking about 15 years.
The experience for women of the death of their mother, then,
is shifting from an event of the middle years to an event
occurring in the immediate pre-retirement years, and is
becoming more predictable in the sense that the duration of
the transition is shortening.

I suspect that a major life cycle transition -- the sort
that our society recognizes as moving people from one
category to another -- requires two things. First, I suspect
it requires a concatenation of separate life cycle events,
and second that those events occur to a cohort over a fairly
brief duration. Demographic changes in the age at death of
one's parents may well be contributing to such a concatenation and to the development of a major life cycle transition
which will be of growing distinctiveness and importance in
the future.

The purpose of this paper has been to describe a demographic view of the life cycle. I have tried to describe
how life cycle notions and facts are related to the central
ideas of demography and to its raison d'être. I am prepared
to admit that this view is a narrow one compared to the
human and social importance of the life course. But perhaps
such narrowness is a necessary price for the intradisciplinary coherence which yields usable meanings. On these grounds
I have not tried to re-write a venerable discipline and
describe a life course view of demography but have rather
sought to foster a broader view by using the demographic
engine to reveal aspects and facts about the life course
which may be uniquely visible from the demographer's vantage
point.

References

1. Lotka, Alfred J.,Orphanhood in relation to demographic
   factors, Metron (Rome) 9: 37-109 (1931).
2. Goodman, Leo A., Keyfitz, Nathan, and Pullum, Thomas W.,
   Family formation and the frequency of various kinship
   relationships. Theoretical Population Biology 5:1-27
   (1974).
3. _____, Addendum to "Family formation and the frequency
   of various kinship relationships." Theoretical Population
   Biology 8:376-381 (1975).
4. Keyfitz, Nathan, Applied Mathematical Demography (Wiley,
   New York, 1977), 273-278.
5. Jacobson, Paul H., Cohort survival for generations since
   1840. Milbank Memorial Fund Quarterly 42:36-53 (1964).

Part 2

Disciplines and Exemplary Populations

5. The Life Course of College Professors and Administrators

We have studied the adult life course of two clearly-defined groups of academic men:

1. Male Sociologists and Psychologists.

2. Male College Administrators (mainly Presidents)

We have questionnaire data and personality test data on these men who were born between 1893 and 1903. For our study we chose only men who had been academically active and at the peak of their careers during the age period 45-60. Most of our information comes from a lengthy questionnaire these men answered in 1975, including two personality tests. The questionnaire was focussed on their lives from age 60-75, though an overview of their early and middle adult careers is also given by the questionnaire.

Our principal question was--how did these men cope with the 60-75 year period in their lives? We find differences between the professors and the administrators, and we find several different subgroups within each of the two main groups. A subordinate question was--how do the professors compare with the administrators in their early life and in their careers leading up to age 60?

The careers of these men can be described in terms of four stages:

I. Choosing and starting a career, age 20-35. This period includes graduate education, leading in most cases to the Ph.D. degree. There were early jobs as college teachers.

II. Career advancement, age 30-50. This period is devoted to teaching, combined with research and writing for some of the men, and promotion to the peak career status.

Table 1.   DESCRIPTION OF THE STUDY GROUP

	Social Scientists		Educators
	B	A	
Total number of qualified men in age group from 1960 Directories		779	323
Number found to have published at age 59-63	343		
Number selected at random from non-publishers	117		
Number in sample to be studied		460	
Number found to be deceased or not locatable		51	91
Number of questionnaires mailed		409	232
Responded to questionnaire		166	110
Reported "too ill" or deceased		40	5
Returned by Post Office as not deliverable		51	22
Response Rate (percent)		166/318 52	110/205 53

Some of the men became internal administrators--department
chairmen and deans. Those who were aiming at an administrative career became college presidents or deans.

III. Career peak, age 50-65. The professors concentrated
on teaching, and on research and publication. The administrators carried on as presidents, in most cases, but a few
served as deans of colleges of engineering, business, law,
or social service. And a small number took leading roles in
the administration of higher education, as officers of national educational organizations.

IV. Approach and adjustment to retirement, age 60-75.
During this period, subgroups emerge and are studied intensively.

THE MEN WHO WERE STUDIED

The names of the men to be studied were obtained from
Directories published close to 1960 or immediately after
that year. The education administrators were identified
through the Directory of American College Presidents and
Deans, 1962-63. Presidents of small church-related colleges were sampled randomly so as to avoid over-weighting
the sample at this status level. Deans of complex universities were included. In the end, 75 college and university
presidents responded fully to the questionnaire, together
with 26 deans and 9 leaders in national educational organizations.

The social scientists were listed in the Directory of
the American Sociological Association, Directory of the
American Psychological Association, or American Men of
Science: The Social and Behavioral Sciences. Only men who
were clearly psychologists or sociologists were included.
This procedure produced 779 names of men whose careers were
definitely in colleges or universities for the years when
they were 45 to 60 years old.

These names were then looked up in the abstracting
journals and the Library of Congress National Union Catalog
to find out whether they had published something during
their 59-63 age period. This procedure produced 343 names
of men who had published, and 436 who had not published in
that age period. Of the "non-publishers," a random sample
of 117 was drawn, on a stratified proportional basis to be
comparable in age and discipline to the "publishers."

As seen in Table 1, 52 percent of the social scientists,
and 53 percent of the educators who received the question-

naire responded. It was important to determine as far as possible how representative the respondents were of the total group who were alive and well in 1975-76, when the study was made. To do this, a brief questionnaire was sent to all non-respondents, asking a number of questions identical with those of the long questionnaire, but requiring only 15 or 20 minutes' time. Those who responded to the brief questionnaire did not differ in any major way from the full-questionnaire respondents.

COMPARISONS OF THE SOCIAL SCIENTISTS AND EDUCATORS

We will report some comparisons of the two groups according to family background and career experience. This will show a rather general similarity.

Area of Residence, Age 5-17. The highest percentage of both groups grew up in the North Central section of the United States: 42 percent of social scientists and 36 percent of educators. A few more educators grew up in the Northeast: 26 percent of educators and 16 percent of social scientists.

Religious Background. Both groups were overwhelmingly Protestant: 91 percent of the educators and 79 percent of the social scientists. But there were no Jews among the educators, while 6 percent of the social scientists were Jewish. Roman Catholics were similar in numbers: 4 percent of the educators and 3 percent of the social scientists.

Father's Occupational Status. For both groups, father's occupations were middle-class to high status. On a 7-point scale of occupational prestige, 77 percent of educators and 72 percent of social scientists had fathers in the upper 3 levels. Among the educators, 27 percent were sons of farmers and 16 percent were sons of clergymen. Among the social scientists, 39 percent were sons of farmers and 18 percent were sons of clergymen. Most of the farmer-fathers were farm owners, and definitely of middle-class socioeconomic status. It will be noted that these men were born around 1900, when the United States economy had a relatively high proportion of farm owners.

Status of Institutions Served at Age 60. As would be expected, the institutions served by the educators varied over a wide range of status, since they were deliberately selected from the entire range, except for junior colleges. On the other hand, the social scientists tended to be located (at age 60) in the higher status institutions. They were at the peak of their careers, which often took them from obscure colleges to higher status institutions as they grew older. On the Carnegie Commission's 5-point scale of institutional status, 69 percent of the social scientists were in the top two categories, compared with 29 percent of the educational administrators. Only 6 percent of the social scientists were in the bottom two categories, compared with 22 percent of the educators.

APPROACHING RETIREMENT

Age at Formal Retirement. Educators retired formally somewhat earlier than social scientists: 47 percent of the educators compared with 32 percent of the social scientists had retired by age 66. This reflected a rather common tendency to retire college presidents at age 65, while college professors might reach mandatory retirement at 67 to 70. Sixty percent of the professors retired at 67-70, compared with 45 percent of the educators.

Fractions of Time Working for Pay. Both groups, as groups, tended to move from working full-time to working part-time for pay, rather than changing abruptly from full-time work to zero compensation. Part-time work might seem to be more accessible to college teachers than to college presidents, but this group of college administrators did find such work, some as professors, some as consultants, some in part-time leadership positions in church or civic welfare organizations. At age 71-72, educators were 17 percent in full-time employment, 40 percent part-time and 43 percent with no paid work. This was quite similar to the situation of social scientists, with a record of 20-36-44.

Feelings on Approach of Retirement. When asked to describe their feelings on the approach of retirement, the administrators reported more favorable feelings: 57 percent said they were "happy about it," compared with 38 percent of social scientists. The latter were more likely to report "mixed feelings" (46 vs. 35 percent) or to have "misgivings" (5 vs. 2 percent).

ADJUSTMENT TO RETIREMENT

Our principal interest in this study is the nature of the process of moving from the peak of a career at age 60 to complete retirement around the age of 75. We wish to compare college administrators with college teachers, and we also expect to find visibly different patterns within each of the two large groups. We shall now report on the process of retirement for sub-groups of the major groups.

Sub-groups Among College Administrators*

The educators reported in the questionnaire rather
fully on their activities in the period from age 65 to 74,
thus providing a basis for scores on a rating scale for professional leadership activity. The rating scale was applied
to two successive periods--65-69 and 70-74 years of age.
This scale gave equal weights to three separate components:
(1) quantitative level of professional activity; (2) new
assignments or positions involving leadership; and (3) leadership activity in the civic, religious, or political arena.
Two judges, working independently, rated a sample of cases.
A Pearson product-moment correlation on this set of scores
for the age range 65 to 69 computed to be .78, and for the
age range 70 to 74 computed to be .90.

Comparison of the score of each man for 65-69 with his
score for 70-74 provided a basis for placing those men into
four life-style sub-groups. A group of 31 percent are
called Maintainers. They held onto an average level of professional activity, generally taking part-time assignments
after formal retirement, and adding other related professional activities to fill their time. An equal-sized group,
called Reducers, dropped in their leadership scores from
65-69 to the 70-74 period. Their comments often indicated
that events made it difficult or unsatisfactory to keep on
with a heavy load of professional work. "I was tired of
the continued routine I had followed in the President's
office for 25 years, but I was sorry to lose touch with
students and colleagues." "I had a light stroke, and con-
cluded I had better relax." A small, 11 percent group, are
called Reorganizers. With great energy and initiative, they
find new forms of leadership. One man, retiring as president of a state university at age 65, entered the federal
government at a high administrative level and held this post
for 7 years. Almost in a class by himself was James Bryant
Conant, who left the university to become Ambassador to Ger-
many, and thereafter organized major studies of the American
High School and of the Preparation of Teachers, which exerted a major influence on public education. He continued to
work in a leadership role into his 80s.

A most unusual group, called Transformers, changed
their life styles radically at age 65 or even earlier

---

* For a detailed report on the educators, see "Life Style
Types and Patterns of Retirement of Educators," by Robert
B. Snow and Robert J. Havighurst.

by choosing a different area of activity. One of these men wrote a note, accompanying his questionnaire: "My post-retirement activity represents a relatively sharp change of the content of my experience. At the time of my full retirement, I was confronted by a series of invitations and opportunities to engage in continued professional work in various cities and as far away as Taiwan. On reflection, my wife and I decided to reject all of them. I had had more than enough of riding in airplanes and living in hotels and we wished to stay here among our good friends. This would give me opportunity to activate a long smouldering interest in painting. The painting now claims my primary interest and labor, and I have become President of our local Art League." There are 26 percent in this group.

Sub-groups Among Social Scientists

For a closer examination of the college professors, we focussed on their <u>publication</u> activities during their 60-75 age period. To secure a <u>Publication Score</u>, a publication list was compiled for each respondent by consulting <u>Psychological Abstracts</u>, <u>Sociological Abstracts</u>, and the <u>Library of Congress National Union Catalog</u> covering the period when the respondent was aged 59 through 73. Weights for various types of publication ranged from 50 points for sole authorship of a book down to 15 points for authorship of a research article, literature review, or a chapter in a book. A publication score was computed for each of five age-intervals: 59-61, 62-64, 65-67, 68-70, 71-73. Scores for each interval were translated into scale scores ranging from 0 to 3 as follows: no publication, 0; 15-25, 1; 26-50, 2; 51 and over, 3. Thus a respondent had five age-interval publication scores. The four age interval scores from 59-70 were added to give a <u>total publication</u> score that ranged from 0 to 12. The age-interval from 71-73 was not included in the total publication score, because the youngest respondents, in 1975, were aged 72 (born in 1903) and could not have a complete score for the 71-73 age period.

<u>Other evidence of professional visibility</u>. Two other scores were obtained for these men, a <u>Citation Score</u> and a <u>Research Grants Score</u>. The Citation Score was based on citations of the man's publications in publications appearing in 1974 and giving a credit for each citation of a publication which appeared when the author was 60 through 71 years of age. Research Grants received by the respondent since age 60 were scored for magnitude. The three scores for professional activity were found to correlate with coefficients of .33, .35, and .46 between the three pairs; grants vs. citations,

Table 2.   DISTRIBUTION OF MALE SOCIAL SCIENTISTS
            IN THE STUDY GROUP BY PUBLICATION SCORE

	Group	Total Score	Number
Low	4 zeros	0	34
	3 zeros	1	25
		— — —	— — —
Middle Group		2-4	16
		5	17
		6-8	21
		— — —	— — —
		9-10	20
High	3 highs	11	12
	4 highs	12	15
			———
			160

Publication score ranges from 0 to 3 for each of
the age-periods: 59-61; 62-64; 65-67; 68-70.
Maximum is 12.

publications vs. citations, and publications vs. grants
respectively.

Study of Publication Sub-groups

The principal measure of professional activity of male
social scientists after age 60 is the publication score.
Table 2 shows how the group members were distributed on publication scores at the age of 70. We have defined three
groups--a low, middle, and high publication group. In the
low group there are 59 men, 37 percent of the Sample, who
did not publish at all between 59 and 70 years of age, or
who published one research article or chapter in a book.
These were mainly the random sample of non-publishers who
had been selected to round out the study group.

The high publication group consists of 47 men who were
consistently "high publishers" throughout their 60s. Fifteen of them scored the maximum (3 points in each of the
four age-intervals), another 12 scored "high" in three age-
intervals and "medium" in the fourth interval; and 20 scored
9 or 10 points, which meant at least two "high" scores and
two other scores adding to 4 or 3.

This left a middle publication group of 54 men with
scores of 2 to 8, spread over the four age intervals.

From the data shown in this Table, supported by qualitative data from the Questionnaire, one can conclude that
there is a substantial degree of <u>continuity</u> in the life
style of the male social scientist, viewed from the age of
60 to the early 70s. A considerable group, about 30 percent
of the men who were studied, are consistently "high publishers." A contrasting group, 37 percent of the men who
were studied, are consistently "low-publishers." (This
group is actually much larger among the total group of male
social scientists, since it is made up almost entirely of
the random sample of non-publishers, who were 436 of the
779 men originally identified as ones who did not publish
between the ages of 59 and 63.) A middle group of 34 percent of the respondents are "middle-level publishers," who
are more variable, a few having achieved a "high" score in
one of the four age intervals, with lower scores in the
other intervals.

<u>Comparison of High and Low Publishers</u>. Two contrasting life
styles emerge when the High and Low publishers are compared
in terms of their responses to several areas of the Questionnaire. We will report a number of findings in terms of per-
centages of the contrasting groups, without indicating the
statistical reliability of the comparisons. In general, a

Table 3.   DIFFERENCES BETWEEN HIGH AND LOW PUBLISHERS
           IN SOURCES OF SELF-ESTEEM

Main sources of self-esteem at time of Responding to Questionnaire*	Percent in Each Subgroup of Publishers	
	High	Low
Approval by colleagues nationwide	70	27
Approval by local colleagues	11	48
Approval by local community	4	35
My research and writing	70	43
My leadership experience	6	40
Attention given my books and speeches	66	18
Awards and prizes	6	5
Approval of my family	28	50
My financial status	9	22
Number of persons in group	(47)	(59)
Number of persons not responding	(5)	(2)

* Respondent was asked to indicate 3 sources. Therefore
each column adds to slightly less than 300 percent, because a few respondents indicated only 2 sources.

difference of 15 to 20 percentage points is reliable at the
5 percent level for two groups of approximately 50 members.

High publishers were more likely to settle early on
their career choice and continue their higher education in
an unbroken and rapid progression, which enabled them to
become established in their career at a much younger age.
Low publishers graduated from college at a later age, and a
number of them taught school before completing their graduate work. The Low publishers were significantly more likely
to become department chairmen or deans than their more re-
search-oriented colleagues. The High publishers on the
other hand were more likely to become president of a professional organization (38 percent vs. 15 percent). High publishers were more likely to be found in the most prestigious
institutions (38 percent vs. 25 percent in the highest status
category). The institutional status measure comes from the
Carnegie Commission on Higher Education's classification of
institutions of higher education, with ranks of 5 (high)
down to 1 (low). The mean status rating for the High publishers was 4.6, and 3.8 for Low publishers.

We have seen that the Low publishers started their careers later and now we find that they also end their careers
sooner: 48 percent of the Low publishers as contrasted with
36 percent of the High publishers worked less than full time
at 69-70, while 30 percent of the High publishers compared
with 14 percent of the Low publishers still held full time
employment after the age of 70. Low publishers were more
likely than High publishers (31 percent vs. 15 percent) to
retire voluntarily from the work role.
A significant finding is reported in Table 3 from the
Questionnaire item asking respondents to indicate three main
sources of their self-esteem. The High publishers pay significantly more attention to the approval of their national
colleagues (70 percent vs. 27 percent), whereas the Low publishers are more oriented to a local reference group (48
percent vs. 11 percent) for approval by local colleagues
and (35 percent vs. 4 percent) for approval by the local
community. High publishers are much more likely to view
their research and writing (70 percent vs. 43 percent) as
an important source of self-esteem, together with "my books
and speeches" (66 percent vs. 18 percent). It is interesting
that "my leadership experience" is favored by the Low publishers (40 percent to 6 percent), probably because they are
local leaders in a variety of situations.

To summarize these varied types of evidence, it appears
that the Low publishers are more aware of and sensitive to
the immediate social environment in which they live and work

Table 4. PERSONALITY SCORES OF EDUCATORS AND MALE SOCIAL SCIENTISTS

MEAN SCORES

Personality Variable	Male Social Scientists Publication Level					Educators		
	High	Medium	Low	Total	SD	Main Group	SD	Transformers
Life Satisfaction	27.8	28.8	28.7	28.5	5.3	29.3	4.1	31.4
Social Extroversion	20.4	19.3	20.6	20.1	6.6	22.7	5.6	23.1
Complexity	13.6	14.4	13.2	13.7	5.6	10.1	4.5	9.4
Practical Outlook	8.7	5.8	8.8	7.8	5.3	10.8	5.0	12.8
Low Anxiety Level	16.4	16.1	17.5	16.8	3.5	17.5	2.6	18.3
Aggressiveness	37.2	37.3	36.6	37.0	6.0	36.9	6.1	37.8
Theoretical Orientation	44.9	43.9	42.7	43.7	7.1	39.6	5.7	39.3
Emotional Stability	46.4	47.2	47.6	47.1	7.4	49.2	7.6	51.0
Personal Integration	44.2	43.3	42.8	43.4	6.1	43.6	5.6	45.0
Warmth and Sociability	48.2	47.4	47.6	47.7	7.2	50.0	7.9	50.7
Self-Sufficiency	37.7	37.4	34.6	36.3	6.6	32.2	6.1	31.5
Number	37	41	53	131		81		29

with a stronger orientation towards a local reference group. The High publishers, on the other hand, are driven by more internal and even abstract motivations; they search for creativity and new experience, but are not dependent on the support of their immediate personal environment.

Personality and Life Style Differences

Since there are major life-style differences among the sub-groups of social scientists, one might expect differences between sub-groups in personality qualities which are measured by personality tests. Table 4 provides data on a number of personality traits, separated out for the three publication sub-groups and including the educational administrators, the latter being separated into two sub-groups-- the Transformers and the Main body. In discussing the personality differences and similarities, we will not systematically report the statistical reliabilities of the differences between various sub-groups. These can be inferred by comparing the actual difference between any two sub-groups with the Standard Deviation of the array of scores. Even though the numbers of men in the various sub-groups are small, there are some differences between sub-groups as large as one-half SD. Also, there are a number of smaller differences on some of the personality traits which point in the direction of a certain conclusion when they are taken together, and which would not have shown this degree of agreement if the differences were accidental in direction and size.

Description of the Personality Tests. The personality tests have been adapted from two well-known sources. One is the Omnibus Personality Inventory, for the variables: Social Extroversion, Complexity, Practical Outlook, Anxiety Level, Theoretical Orientation and Personal Integration. The other is the Cattell 16 PF Inventory for the variables Warmth and Sociability, Self-Sufficiency, Emotional Stability, and Aggressiveness.[2]

---

2 The Omnibus Personality Inventory was designed originally for use with college students. A few of the items were clearly not suited to elderly professors, and were replaced by more suitable items in the same categories. The four Cattell 16 PF Traits were adapted to a Q sort, or Self-Sort Inventory, together with Theoretical Orientation and Personal Integration from the OPI. A more detailed description is given in the extended Report, Lives After Sixty.

Very brief descriptions of these personality variables
are:
Aggressiveness. Self-assertive, dominating, vs. self-criti-
cal, modest, submissive.

Theoretical Orientation. Sees the essence of a problem, prefers dealing with theoretical concerns, vs. not interested
in research, dislikes intensive study.

Emotional Stability. Realistic, stable, practical, vs.
changeable, tense, excitable.

Personal Integration. Well-organized, communicates easily
with others, feels comfortable with himself, vs. bothered
by certain thoughts and ideas, feels as though he is drift-
ing through life.

Warmth and Sociability. Outgoing, cooperative, genial, vs.
withdrawn, aloof, cold.

Self-Sufficiency. Independent, prefers to work alone, intro-
spective, vs. gregarious, tactful, sensitive to needs of
others.

The OPI traits of Social Extroversion, Complexity, Practical
Outlook, and Anxiety Level hardly need further description.
It should be noted in using Table 4 that a high score on
Anxiety Level means a low anxiety level.

Personality Traits That Differentiate Social Scientists From Educators

We may look first in Table 4 at the differences between
the Educators and the Social Scientists. It will be noted
that wherever the Educators differ appreciably from the
Social Scientists, the Transformers are at one extreme, beyond the Main Group of Educators.

Social Extroversion. The Educators are more outgoing and
people oriented than the Social Scientists.

Complexity. The Social Scientists have much higher scores
on the dimension of complexity. This represents an experimental and flexible orientation. Both in their research and
in their teaching, they must analyze complex phenomena, and
always be prepared to say "It is not so simple" when dealing
with students or administrators.

Practical Outlook. The Educators have a more practical outlook, with what that term implies for working on problems and
issues in a complex situation like a university.

Anxiety Level. Educators have a somewhat lower anxiety level, amounting to about one-third of a Standard Deviation.
Both groups have a relatively low anxiety level, since the
highest possible score on the test is 20, and a number of
respondents score at that level of low anxiety. Still, it
appears that the social scientists have slightly more feelings of anxiety or self-doubt.

Theoretical Orientation. Social scientists have a much higher degree of theoretical orientation than college administrators, since this quality is central to their teaching and
their research activity.

Emotional Stability. The administrators appear to have
somewhat greater emotional stability.

Warmth and Sociability. Administrators have a greater degree
of sociability.

Self-Sufficiency. The most striking difference between the
two broad groups lies in the quality of Self-Sufficiency,
where the social scientists exceed the educators by two-
thirds of a standard deviation. This is to be expected,
since the social scientists who conduct research and write
articles must do a good deal of work alone. While administrators give speeches and some of them write books, they
are less likely to devote extended periods of time to lone
activity.

Personality Traits That Differentiate High From Low
Publishers Among Social Scientists

    Looking at the personality trait scores for the High
Publishers and the Low Publishers, we detect only two that
seem to show significant differences, Theoretical Orientation and Self-Sufficiency. These both go in the direction
one would expect, knowing that the Low Publishers have had
more varied careers, including a variety of work experience
before obtaining the Ph.D. degree, and more positions as
department chairman or dean of a liberal arts college or
division. The High Publishers have spent more of their
adult career in concentrated research and related teaching.
The difference between the two groups in Self-Sufficiency
is almost half of the Standard Deviation.

DISCUSSION

The most general conclusion from our study of the life course of university and college administrators and professors of social science is that the career pattern which reached its peak of activity and influence at the age of 45 to 60 continues through the age period of 60 to 75 in a fairly predictable way. The advent of formal retirement requires some adaptation for administrators, and they use their energy and initiative to keep active in roles built on their pre-retirement careers. Of the four definable sub-groups among the administrators, only one, the Transformer role, is sharply discontinuous for 25 percent of the administrators.

The sociology and psychology professors exhibit a great deal of continuity with their career activity at age 60. Based on a measurement of their publication record, we find that those who are High Publishers at about age 60 continue to be high on into their early 70s, while those who are Low or Zero Publishers at about age 60 continue at that level. However, the Low Publishers have established satisfactory and useful career patterns with more administrative responsibility and people-oriented activity. The men with Low Publication records are as well satisfied with their careers as those with High Publication records, but the two sub-groups get their sense of self-esteem from different reference groups. Although the Low Publishers have more administrative responsibility and are more people-oriented than the High Publishers, they are still social science professors, and differ in personality more from college administrators than they do from the more research oriented social science professors.

We may define a concept of <u>dependence on the social environment</u> for goals and clues to action, as opposed to a concept of <u>dependence on ideas</u>, together with <u>skill</u> and <u>interest in cognitive analysis and structuring</u> of the environment.

With this definition we see the administrators as attached to the social environment, while the High Publishing social scientists are more independent of their social environment. The Low Publishing social scientists, then, are between these two opposite poles of interest and activity.

NOTE

This Research has been aided financially by the National Institute of Child Health and Human Development, Grant No. PHS 5-Rol HD-08879-02. Details of the methods and findings of this research are contained in a 120-page off-set publication entitled Social Scientists and Educators: Lives After Sixty, which is available for $2.50 (the cost of preparation and mailing) from Robert J. Havighurst, Department of Education, University of Chicago, Chicago, IL. 60637. This includes a parallel study of female social scientists, and of male college and university administrators.

REFERENCES

Cattell, R.B., Eber, H.W., and Tatsuoka, M.M. Handbood for the sixteen personality factor questionnaire (16PF). Champaign, IL. Institute for Personality and Ability Testing. 1970.

Havighurst, R.J., McDonald, W.J., Perun, P.J., and Snow, R.B. Social Scientists and Educators: Lives after Sixty. Chicago: University of Chicago, Committee on Human Development. 1976

Heist, P., and Yonge, G. The omnibus personality inventory, Form E. Manual. New York: Psychological Corporation. 1968.

Snow, Robert B. and Havighurst, Robert J. Life Style Types and Patterns of Retirement of Educators. Gerontologist, 1977, 17, 545-552.

Pamela J. Perun, Denise Del Vento Bielby

6. Structure and Dynamics of the Individual Life Course

Conceptual elaboration of the complexity of the life course has proven to be a difficult task for human developmentalists since the emergence of a perspective concerned with growth and change throughout the life span. In an attempt to integrate the number of discrete life stages previously defined in the literature into a dynamic and continuous unity, recent work by Baltes (1), Baltes and Willis (2), Mortimer and Simmons (3), and Runyan (4) has emphasized the importance of a multivariate and multi-disciplinary approach, both theoretically and methodologically, to the study of the life course. Although it is now accepted that the life course emerges as a consequence of a dynamic interaction between the individual, the immediate environment and the social structure, there is as yet no model in the literature of our contemporary understanding of the structure of individual lives.

There is a similar and related gap in the conceptualization of the basic mechanisms underlying developmental processes throughout the life span. A serious obstacle to theoretical advancement has been the difficulty in isolating a single mechanism to account for both stability and change in developmental phenomena over time. In this regard, the concept of timing as discussed by Neugarten and Hagestad (5) has received considerable attention in recent years, as has Riegel's (6) conceptualization of synchronicity as a theoretical elaboration of timing. Yet, the usefulness of these concepts for the specification of developmental processes is virtually unexplored and their integration into a unified theory of life span development remains relatively incomplete.

Our intention in this paper is therefore twofold. We first discuss the theoretical and methodological importance

of timing and synchronicity to analysis of developmental processes by briefly tracing their conceptual evolution in the
literature. We then illustrate their relevance to the specification of developmental processes through the presentation of a model of individual development in which synchronicity plays a critical role in defining both the structure
and content of the individual life course. Applications and
implications of the model for empirical research are discussed in the final section of the paper through an analysis of the life histories of an early generation of academic
women social scientists.

Conceptual Background of the Model

Within the literature on life span development exists
a loosely-defined school of thought which views timing as a
pivotal mechanism regulating the life course of individuals.
Adherents of this school, a diverse group of sociologists,
psychologists and clinicians, view development as paced at
the level of the individual by a sense of an "average, expectable life cycle" (7). In Butler's view, this "individual
inner sense of the life cycle"

> is neither the same as the average expectable life
> cycle nor the same as a personal sense of identity,
> although it is related to both. It is a subjective
> feel for the life cycle as a whole, its rhythm, its
> variability, and the relation of this to the indivi-
> dual's sense of himself. This inner sense seems to
> be a necessary personal achievement in order for the
> individual to orient himself wherever he happens to
> be on the life cycle (8).

Similarly, Neugarten has discussed how this phenomenon of a
sense of the "normal, expectable life-cycle" evolves within
the individual in relation to timing.

> Adults carry around in their heads, whether or not
> they can easily verbalize it, a set of anticipa-
> tions of the normal, expectable life-cycle. They
> internalize expectations of the consensually-vali-
> dated sequences of major life events - not only
> what those events should be, but when they should
> occur. They make plans and set goals along a time-
> line shaped by these expectations (9).

According to Neugarten, achievement of that inner sense of
self in time is itself a function of life experience in that
"it is perhaps not until adulthood that the individual creates a sense of the life-cycle; that is, an anticipation and

acceptance of the inevitable sequence of events that will occur as men grow up, grow old and die - in adulthood, that he understands that the course of his own life will be similar to the lives of others, and that the turning points are inescapable" (10).

The development of such an inner sense of time and its passage reflects the reciprocal relationship between individual lives and the social structure in which they are embedded. Through a system of age norms, the social structure establishes time boundaries regulating the individual's passage through life. In Neugarten's view, "the age norm system not only provides mechanisms for allocating new recruits to major social roles; it also creates an ordered and predictable life course; it creates timetables, and it sets boundaries for acceptable behavior at successive life stages" (11). As a consequence of these often nonverbal timing norms, the individual internalizes an expected pattern of life events which becomes translated into a personal sense of the structure and rhythm of the course of his or her own life. Thus, time at both the individual and social levels of analysis is a critical mechanism regulating the course of life. For the individual, the timing of events in the life course has both social and psychological consequences. As Neugarten has shown, "a psychology of the life cycle is not a psychology of crisis behavior so much as it is a psychology of timing" (12).

In recent theoretical statements, Riegel (6, 13, 14) has considerably extended the role of timing in a multi-dimensional conceptualization of human development. He postulates in his dialectical theory of development four levels of human organization which interact simultaneously: inner-biological; individual-psychological; cultural-sociological; and outer-physical. In Riegel's view,

A dialectical interpretation of human development always considers at least two concurrent temporal sequences ... taken separately, these sequences are mere abstractions. Development results from the synchronization of any two and indirectly of all these progressions. Developmental leaps are brought about by lack of coordination and represent major forms of reorganizations ... they provide the fundamental basis for the development of the individual and for the history of society (15).

Riegel's conceptualization extends beyond the boundaries of the individual life course to include multiple dimensions

of human existence in simultaneous and interactive operation.
Concerned with the totality of development as a result of
the multi-dimensional interplay of biological, psychological,
cultural, and historical processes, he clearly considers synchronicity to be a fundamental mechanism of development.
Through his theoretical reformulations, Riegel has therefore
directed our attention to a more complex view of human development as a composite of multiple time sequences, each related to a particular schematic dimension.

As a result, traditional ideas about time as a uni-di-
mensional concept in human development are now inadequate.
Given the necessity to consider a multiplicity of time sequences, each representing simultaneous progressions of
events, conceptualization of the coordination of such sequences both singly and in relation to others becomes increasingly important. That is, our understanding of the
life course now encompasses a multiplicity of times, or
timetables, whose coordination becomes a major focus of
developmental research. Hence, it is imperative that developmentalists consider the implications of a multi-level
conceptualization of time and begin to examine issues of synchrony and asynchrony in the individual life course. As
Riegel has written, development is never a static event;
rather,

> development ... consists in continuous changes.
> Critical points occur and can be regarded as
> transitions between stages whenever two sequences
> are out of step, i. e., when synchronization
> breaks down. Asynchronies and contrasts are
> the basis for developmental progressions. Stable
> plateaus of balance or tranquility are the excep-
> tion ... Development requires a delicate syn-
> chrony between different progressions. Synchro-
> nization is comparable to balance, but it is a
> balance in change which requires continuous ef-
> forts and actions within the various dimensions
> interacting in developmental progressions (16).

Independent of the merits of Riegel's particular theory of development, it is clear that his introduction of
synchronicity as a developmental concept represents a so-
phisticated elaboration of the meaning of time to the individual life course which increases our ability to understand
the complexity of human development. As Eichorn (17) has
shown, previous references to synchrony and asynchrony in
the literature have been limited to discussions of uncoordi-
nated physical growth curves. Empirical research into social-psychological or social- structural correlates of syn-

chronization of developmental processes has been minimal. Thus, it is now appropriate to specify a theoretical framework in which synchronicity plays a major role in determining the structure and content of the individual life course.

A Model of
the Individual Life Course:
Structure and Dynamics

The model proposed here is built upon a multi-dimensional conception of time as a fundamental regulatory mechanism in human development. Rooted within the same theoretical tradition as Neugarten's empirical work and Riegel's dialectical schema, it differs in important ways from earlier work through its focus on the individual life course with minimal consideration at this time of biological, cultural or historical timing sequences. By narrowing its focus to the complex set of developmental processes comprising the individual life course, the model provides a conceptual framework for analyzing growth and change in individual lives from birth to death.

The following assumptions underlie the model depicted in Figure 1. First, time in this model is not synonymous with chronological age, that is, with time since birth. Following Baer (18) and Wohlwill (19), it is assumed that chronological age "causes" nothing. Chronological age is only an idiosyncratic marker of movement through time. Second, although the legitimacy of chronological age as an explanatory variable is increasingly dubious, time in an absolute sense remains a fundamental developmental concept. Further, time in a relative sense is useful as a system of notation of movement through developmental processes. Third, the individual life course is composed of multiple dimensions developmental in nature in that they are principally characterized by non-random growth or change functions organized in a temporal sequence. Hence, we posit that the individual life course is a composite structure of multiple dimensions exhibiting a multiplicity of timetables, each corresponding to a particular dimension and to movement through that dimension. We thus assert that the fundamental regulatory mechanism of the individual life course is synchronicity, that is, the degree of coordination displayed by a multiplicity of timetables relative to each other at a given point in time. Finally, it is assumed that the individual life course is also a whole structural unit internally regulated according to the degree of synchronicity displayed by its constituent dimensions.

Before defining the content of our model, it is first

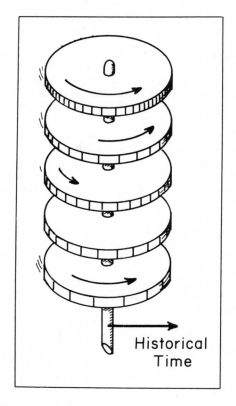

Figure 1.   A model of the individual life course.

useful to discuss its structure. Our use of the construct "structure" in relation to the individual life course establishes its unity as equal to more than the sum of its parts. As Loevinger has noted, structure implies that

> (1) there are many elements or parts, and (2) that these elements are not simply an aggregate ... but are related to each other so as to form a well-defined order ... in each case the structure consists of the set of relations among the elements. These relations provide the unity and give each element meaning as a part of the whole. When the basic relations change, the structure changes. On the other hand, ... all the elements may change without the structure changing (20).

The structure of this model refers to the boundaries of the progressions, or dimensions, of which the life course is composed, thus representing the relationship of an individual life to time measured in an absolute sense within history.

Within that structure each of the constituent dimensions is in simultaneous operation, moving in time at a rate specific to itself. Because dimensions in the model are specified to be dynamic, each by definition consists of a developmental progression in which antecedents, sequelae, and transitions serve as markers of passage. Our definition of a developmental dimension thus builds on Kohlberg's assertion that the task of developmental research is "to isolate a function, ... and to define it by a progressive developmental clarification of the functions", (21) by moving from consideration of a single function to the simultaneous consideration of many. In short, this model of the individual life course illustrated in Figure One conceptualizes human development as multi-dimensional in content and internally regulated by a multiplicity of timetables.

Although each individual's life course structure may differ in substantial ways from another's in either dimension composition or timing schedules, there are several more or less "universal" dimensions. In the psychological literature, for example, are several well-defined developmental progressions linked to intra-psychic growth and change, the most prominent being Piaget's (22) theory of cognitive development, Loevinger's (20) theory of ego development and Kohlberg's (23) theory of moral development. Although these theorists commonly utilize a stage model to explain development, the phenomena they study also fit our definition of a temporal progression because, by definition, "each stage is a delimited structure ..., fixed in a sequence of structures

but theoretically independent of time and total organismic
state" (24). Although Loevinger (20) has suggested that ego
development is itself composed of multiple dimensions, at
the present time it will be represented in the model as a
single dimension. Thus, in Figure 1, several of the dimensions in the model are hypothesized to be psychological in
nature.

In the sociological literature as well can be found
theoretical constructs which fit our definition of developmental progressions. Such constructs are usually referred
to as "cycles" of life experience, the most commonly accepted
being those organizing the major life dimensions of family
and work into temporal role sequences. In Figure 1, therefore, several of the dimensions are assumed to be dimensions
of life experience characterized by a logical temporal ordering of events in antecedent-sequelae relationships. This
model thus differs considerably from earlier work by Hogan
(25) and Marini (26), among others, who have used a uni-di-
mensional view of time to organize life events in terms of
precedence by chronological age at event, as if the individual life course were composed of a random assortment of
life events. Such an ordering ignores the fact that most
life events (e.g., age at marriage, age at first job, age at
completion of education) are the outcomes of separate developmental processes, although interactions between events
in separate dimensions are to be expected. That is, the logical developmental ordering of events in a causal chain is
within rather than between dimensions. Previous attempts to
model the individual life course by focusing on ages at
events have failed to consider the prior developmental sequences related to those very events. Hence, the specification of cycles of life events in this model is based upon
a conceptualization of development as rooted in a multi-dimensional, rather than a multivariate, life course structure
in which the linkages in series of related events are of primary importance.

The model of the individual life course depicted in
Figure 1 is a structure composed of universal temporal sequences of both psychological and sociological processes.
Each temporal sequence has its own timetable with tolerance
of individual differences in timing dependent upon the nature of the phenomenon in each dimension. Similarly, the
composite of dimensions in a particular individual's life depends on placement in a social structure and within a social
and historical context. The central purpose of the model is
as a useful device for categorizing in a meaningful way differentiated developmental processes simultaneously and for
efficiently organizing life history data which is, after all,

far easier to collect than to analyze. Thus, the primary
function of the model is to aid the researcher in tracing
the movement of an individual along multiple life dimensions.
That is, if one were to halt the dynamic movement of individual life structures at a particular point in time, it
would then be possible to make complex comparisons between
individuals, whether between two thirty year old women or
between a thirty year old man and a sixty year old man, on
a number of important dimensions. It should be noted that
this model does not assume evolution of the life structure
into a more complex configuration over time because increased complexity can be accounted for by the addition of
dimensions. Subtraction of dimensions when completed may
also occur. Further, the number of events or stages comprising a dimension may vary over time and from one individual to another. Thus, the basic structure of the individual life course in this model is hypothesized to remain the
same throughout life although its constituent dimensions may
increase or decrease in complexity due to the intrinsic nature of specific developmental processes.

Because the dynamic nature of the model is a function
of the simultaneous movement of multiple dimensions, the
synchronicity of timetables becomes an important developmental consideration. Synchronicity is defined as the extent
to which the timetables of the dimensions in a particular
life structure proceed in coordination. Asynchrony occurs
when one or more dimensions is off-time in relation to others.
Such mistiming is seen as "friction" within the structure of
dimensions which is perceived by the individual as a state
of crisis and which causes or results in changes in one or
more dimensions until synchronicity, but not homeostasis, is
re-established. For example, a divorce may halt the existing sequence in the family dimension and cause a "re-
winding" of the sequence until forward movement is resumed
through a re-marriage which begins again the family sequence
and re-sets the timing mechanism. Asynchrony can also be
the result of a disruption in a specific sequence of events
with an interactive effect on other timetables as well. For
example, experiencing a life event off-time with the age
norm system may cause considerable disruption in a particular psychological dimension. Because perfect synchrony is
rarely achieved in any life structure, asynchrony between
and within dimensions is, to some degree, a constant feature
of human existence. Its function is therefore to serve as
a mechanism coordinating multiple timetables requiring only
minimal adjustments at some times but massive alterations at
others.

A fundamental assumption of the model is that synchronous movement through developmental progressions is contingent to a large extent on timing schedules established by the social structure with individuals experiencing rewards and punishments both intra-psychically and socially relative to their lives' congruity with externally prescribed age norms. That is, individuals moving on-time through a developmental progression are presumed to experience minimal distortion between their senses of the average, expectable life course and the timings of life events which results in a minimum of asynchrony in their life structures. Individuals moving off-time experience a greater degree of asynchrony within one dimension which may as a result affect the organization of the life structure as a whole. Being off-time may result from both positively and negatively perceived experiences but the consequences are presumed to be similar in magnitude. For example, an athlete or musician may experience professional success at an age when movement through the sequences of cognitive or ego development is out-of-sync with available responsibilities and privileges while a woman beginning a career at age forty-five frequently finds herself out-of-sync with the temporal sequence associated with the work cycle. Although being early and being late may be evaluated differently by outside observers, the resultant lack of coordination may have identical consequences for the affected individuals. It is also possible for many people to experience similar instances of asynchrony. A contemporary example is the large numbers faced with mandatory retirement at an age out-of-sync with their biological or family cycles. As a result of the reciprocal relationship between the social structure and the individual life structure, a revised timetable for the work cycle is currently under consideration in order to reduce the evident asynchrony. Hence, the social structure is responsive, particularly in times of social and historical change, to aggregate changes in developmental timetables as the individual is similarly responsive to changes in the social structure.

This model thus extends and elaborates earlier work on the relationship between timing and development throughout the life span. The structure of the individual life course presented here is an attempt to illustrate a conceptualization of synchrony as a fundamental mechanism of development similar to Riegel's musical metaphor, of which he wrote;

> In polyphonic compositions various sound sequences
> are occasionally in unison, frequently in harmony,
> but most often in tension. Polyphonic composi-
> tions are comparable to networks of event sequences
> that characterize individuals' developments in

their temporal sequences. They are comparable,
for example, to the individuals' attempts to synchronize their wishes with their duties, their
affects with their skills, their movements with
their thoughts.(27)

Our model emphasizes the polyphonic, or multi-dimensional, nature of the individual life course through the coordinate
linkage of previously defined progressions of intra-psychic
development with temporal sequences of life experience traditionally viewed in isolation by the separate disciplines
of psychology and sociology. It represents a developmental
perspective which asserts that the course of life is not
universal, invariant or hierarchical, although specific dimensions within the totality of development may exhibit such
characteristics. It also regards theories of development
proposed by Gould (28) and Levinson (29) which rely on chronological age as a causal mechanism as methodological over-
simplifications of complex processes. Finally, it represents a conceptualization of the life course as the simultaneous operation of multiple time clocks of psychological,
social and biological processes equally complex at birth and
at death. Avoiding the teleological implications of such de-
signs as the "life spiral" (30) this model permits the waxing
and waning in importance of dimensions specific to particular
periods of life while acknowledging the complexity of human
development throughout the life span. In addition, the model
provides an analytical focus for research into life histories
through its ability to specify the "linkages between aspects
of the social structure, personality, and behavior" (30) by
simultaneous consideration of the age norm system, intra-psychic development and cycles of life experience. Thus, the
model of the individual life course presented in this paper
moves work in this tradition from a descriptive to an explanatory mode through its ability to explain both stability and
change from birth to death at the individual as well as at
the aggregate levels of analysis.

Applications of the Model
to Empirical Research

In the remainder of the paper, the usefulness of the model for empirical research will be explored. Our discussion
will by necessity be descriptive in nature, although recent
work by Tuma, Hannan and Groeneveld (32) has clarified the
mathematical problems associated with the statistical analysis
of series of event histories. Our intention is to illustrate
how the model can be used to organize and analyze life history data. Empirical evidence of synchronization of develop-

mental processes is fragmentary; however, our discussion will utilize existing work to highlight certain features of the model and to suggest topics for future research.

In order to illustrate the role of synchronicity in developmental processes, it is useful to examine the life course structure of women because women are in increasing numbers adding a work cycle (33) to their traditional responsibilities as wives and mothers. While the traditional structure of men's lives is also being re-examined through the questioning of sex role stereotypes, issues of synchrony and asynchrony have been minimally addressed. At present, the primary discussion of asynchrony has been limited to Oppenheimer's (34) hypothesis of a "life cycle squeeze" relative to men's earning power in various stages of the work cycle and the family cycle. Hence, the changes in women's lives which are being demonstrated and debated today provide the best evidence of the presence and consequences of asynchrony in life course structures.

The traditional structure of women's lives during the course of this century has been substantially modified, particularly in regard to interactions between family and work event cycles. Although Glick (35) has shown that average ages at specific events in the family cycle have displayed some variability in response to economic and demographic constraints, one constant element in women's lives has nevertheless been the central position of the family cycle. Earlier in this century, a work cycle was of minor importance to the structure of women's lives because it began and ended prior to the real life work of marrying and raising a family. Then, in the post-war years, women began to re-enter the labor force in their 40s and 50s as changes in the timing of the family cycle and increased longevity extended the period of time in which women were freed from major parental responsibilities. Increasingly, the structure of women's lives altered as the major event sequences in family and work assumed a staggered pattern in adulthood. More recently, however, an even more fundamental re-structuring of women's lives has occurred as the family and work cycles have become simultaneous, rather than sequential, components of adulthood.

In terms of our model, the typical life structure of women at the turn of the century can be visualized as one of alternating cycles in which the work cycle was in movement until the family cycle began. A different type of coordination was then adopted by later generations of women in which the work cycle stopped as the family cycle began but was restarted later in life. The emerging life structure of contemporary women is one in which the work and family cycles be-

gin and proceed simultaneously. The consequences of these
fundamental alterations in the structure of women's lives
have not yet been thoroughly understood. In the past, the
structure of men's lives has permitted the simultaneous operation of family and work cycles because women assumed primary
responsibility for family events during the intensive years
of childbearing and childrearing. Now that women have added
a work cycle and economic responsibilities to their traditional life work of wife and mother, the presence and consequences
of asynchronies in individual life structures are becoming increasingly apparent.

   An important consequence of these changes is that asynchronies in life structures between the family and the work
cycles originate at a specific point in the lives of contemporary women. In a study of the timing of parenthood,
Daniels and Weingarten have found that in women's lives "a
transition in the sphere of parenthood and family life almost
invariably led to a shift in the sphere of employed work"
(36). That shift occurred with the birth of the first child
which forced the women studied to make, in Daniels and Weingarten's term, "patterns of accommodation" in order to reach
a solution of the opposed responsibilities of the family and
work cycles in their life structures. It appears that for
contemporary women the birth of the first child triggers a
major internal re-organization of the existing life structure
in an attempt to re-establish a synchronic operation of con-
flicting events in the work and family cycles. Weingarten
and Daniels note that for the husbands studied, "there was
minimal overlap between the spheres of family and employment.
Changes occurred on the job, and changes occurred within
their families, but the changes at home were not usually associated with changes at work. It is as if these changes ...
took place parallel to each other. This is not the case for
the women in the sample" (37). Two patterns of accommodation or, in our terms, resolutions of asynchrony, were a-
dopted by the women studied: (1) a sequential pattern of
halting the work cycle until a later stage in the family cycle; or (2) a simultaneous co-ordination of family and work
cycles. Both patterns were achieved at some cost to the women and with predictable consequences for later re-organiza-
tions of life structures. It is interesting to note that a-
doption of the simultaneous pattern was more typical of col-
lege-educated late mothers, thus suggesting that successful
establishment of a simultaneous pattern of work and family
for women may depend upon earlier investment and rewards from
the work cycle. Given the increasing numbers of mothers with
young children in the labor force, it is apparent that the
simultaneous pattern is becoming more common for contemporary
women. As yet, however, the process by which women come to

Table 1. Mean Ages at Events Among Married Academic Women
Social Scientists (Standard Deviations in Parentheses)

	Patterns of Group A[1] (No Children)		
	I[a]	II[b]	III[c]
Mean Age At Completion of Ph.D	40.5 (7.7)	29.0 (6.1)	32.0 (5.1)
Mean Age At Marriage	26.7 (3.9)	39.0 (6.7)	32.0 (6.1)

	Patterns of Group B[2] (Children)		
	I[a]	II[b]	III[c]
Mean Age At Completion of Ph.D	42.5 (9.0)	28.0 (0.0)	27.7 (3.4)
Mean Age At Marriage	24.8 (3.9)	37.0 (1.4)	25.6 (2.3)
Mean Age At Birth Of First Child	32.7 (6.4)	42.0 (2.8)	31.8 (4.5)

[1]Pattern I (n=10), II (n=6), III (n=5).

[2]Pattern I (n=12), II (n=2), III (n=6).

[a]Sequential Pattern of marriage, then doctorate;

[b]Sequential Pattern of doctorate, then marriage;

[c]Simultaneous Pattern of marriage and doctorate
 at approximately same ages.

re-establish synchrony in their lives after a major disruption such as the birth of the first child and the relative merits of one solution versus another remain important topics for future research.

The patterns of accommodation between work and family demonstrated by the women in the Daniels and Weingarten study are strikingly similar to those exhibited by a pioneer group of highly educated, professional women. In a study of the life histories of academic women social scientists born between 1893 and 1906 (38, 39), there is suggestive evidence of differing strategies of synchronization between family and work cycles by these highly educated women. Analysis of a sub-sample from that study, i. e. women with doctorates who married, reveals several patterns of synchronization. There were 41 women, only 20 of whom had children, in the sub-sample which was divided into two groups for comparative purposes: (a) women with doctorates who married; and (b) women with doctorates who married and had children. In the following comparison, the beginning of the work cycle was arbitrarily defined to be the age at receipt of the doctorate and the family cycle was assigned two sequential events, age at marriage and age at birth of first child. When the groups are compared as a whole, they appear relatively homogeneous. The average age at first marriage for Group A is 31.5 years (S. D. 7.3) and for Group B 27.2 years (S. D. 4.5). The average age at first child for women in Group B was 31.5 years (S. D. 6.3) with an average family size of 1.85 children (S. D. .88). The average age at doctorate for Group A was 35.1 years (S. D. 8.3) and for Group B 36.6 years (S. D. 10.2). However, when comparisons are made across patterns within each group, different strategies of synchronizations emerge.

As shown in Table 1, there were three patterns of synchronization between family and work cycles found within each group: (I) a sequential pattern of marriage, then completion of a doctorate; (II) another sequential pattern of receipt of a doctorate, then marriage; and (III) a simultaneous pattern of marriage and completion of a doctorate. The mean age at each event varies widely according to the pattern of synchronization and reveals greater consistency within patterns than within groups. For women exhibiting Sequential Pattern I or II, the mean age at marriage and the mean age at receipt of the doctorate are nearly identical for Group A and Group B. At the same time, women in Pattern III are very different from women with other patterns, regardless of group placement. For example, among women in Sequential Pattern II, completion of the doctorate is primarily an event of the age decades of the 20s. Among women in Sequential Pattern I, in contrast, com-

Table 2. Status Attainments of Married Academic Women
Social Scientists (Standard Deviations in Parentheses)

	Patterns of Group A[1] (No Children)		
	I[a]	II[b]	III[c]
Mean Status of Ph.D Institution[3]	4.7 (.48)	4.7 (.52)	4.0 (.10)
Mean Status of Institution at Age 60[3]	4.3 (.80)	4.1 (.75)	4.0 (1.2)
Mean Academic Rank At Age 60[4]	4.5 (.70)	4.7 (.52)	5.0 (0.0)
	Patterns of Group B[2] (Children)		
	I[a]	II[b]	III[c]
Mean Status of Ph.D Institution[3]	4.8 (.62)	5.0 (0.0)	5.0 (0.0)
Mean Status of Institution at Age 60[3]	3.7 (.89)	3.5 (2.1)	4.2 (.75)
Mean Academic Rank At Age 60[4]	4.9 (.29)	5.0 (0.0)	5.0 (0.0)

[1]Pattern I (n=10), II (n=6), III (n=5).

[2]Pattern I (n=12), II (n=2), III (n=6).

[3]See Havighurst (40) for ranking scheme.

[4]Professor=5, Associate Professor=4, Assistant Professor=3, Lecturer=2, No Affiliation=1 (no valid cases).

[a]Sequential Pattern of marriage, then doctorate;

[b]Sequential Pattern of doctorate, then marriage:

[c]Simultaneous Pattern of marriage and doctorate at approximately same ages.

pletion of the doctorate occurs during the 30s and 40s, with
no women in this pattern completing the doctorate in the 20s.
Women in Simultaneous Pattern III resemble the "early" timing
of events of the other patterns, having both married and completed professional training at a relatively early age, that
is, in the late 20s and the early 30s on the average. For
these women, an important interaction between cycles appears
to occur with the birth of the first child. Among women in
Sequential Pattern I, the birth of children appears to have
added, on the average, two years to the time span between
marriage and receipt of the doctorate. No such gap is evident for women who synchronized their work and family cycles
differently. Although the numbers in each cell are so small
that any findings must be regarded as tentative, the age differences between and across patterns suggest that the critical element in the structure of these women's lives for later
academic achievement was not having married or having completed a doctorate. Rather, the fundamental difference
among these women was the timing of each event, both within
a particular event series and in relation to other series of
events simultaneously operating in their life structures.
Hence, examination of the patterns of accommodation between
work and family in these women's lives provides preliminary
evidence of the importance of synchronization to the structure of individual lives.

However, in order for the impact of such alternative
patterns of synchronizations to be fully understood, it is necessary to determine their consequences later in life. Previous analyses of these data have demonstrated that marriage
and childbearing per se cannot explain professional advancement among these women scientists (38, 39). As Table 2 il-
lustrates, there are few differences in professional status
achievements, either at the beginning or at the end of the
work cycle, related to alternative synchronization patterns.
Again, inferences from these data must be made with great
caution, but these data suggest that married women, with or
without children, completed their doctorate at high ranking
institutions. Most women became professors, although there
is evidence to suggest that more women who received their
doctorates earlier, on the average, achieved that particular
rank (see also 39). Further, in regard to the status of the
academic institution, there are indications that women with
children were employed at lower ranking institutions at age
60.

Because the study of this early generation of academic
women social scientists was retrospective rather than longitudinal in design, there are few data available on the psychological consequences to these women and their families

of alternative synchronization patterns between work and family cycles. Further, it is strongly suspected that this early cohort of academic women lost many members who could not synchronize family and work cycles successfully. An additional synchronization pattern not represented in these data would thus be found among professionally trained women who abandoned their work completely because of family demands. Therefore, because the patterns found here are not necessarily exhaustive or even representative of the range of possible types of synchronizations, it is difficult at this time to specify causal relationships between resolutions of asynchronizations earlier in time with life course outcomes.

However, anecdotal evidence does provide some clues to the consequences of asynchronies in individual life structures. For one woman in the study, achieving synchrony meant limiting professional training, but not aspirations. She wrote, "I began my teaching on the master's level at [omitted] University. I was 40 years of age. My family had all come safely thru the way and I was reluctant to leave to finish the doctorate. I made closure on the degree in favor of ... family. Many times the degreed prof got the job I was capable of handling!" Another woman clearly limited professional work during her early years because she felt, "I owed much to a child with two Ph.D. parents." Nevertheless, through a fortunate combination of circumstances, she was able to resume her career quite successfully in her fifties and remains, even in her seventies, an active participant in her discipline. Another women faced long periods of asynchronization not only between dimensions but within her work cycle as well. She wrote, "Marriage in 1930 closed teaching field opportunities. I learned business skills - taught them in secretarial school, got a position with a personnel consultant firm - and presto - re-entered psychology as an industrial psychologist. This in turn made me a desirable WAVE officer candidate ... and such are the exigencies of war that by 1945 I emerged as a bona fide clinical psychologist!" Yet, despite its ultimate happy ending, that fifteen year hiatus from her work as a psychologist clearly had adverse professional consequences in terms of her achievements by age sixty. Finally, another woman who reported that marriage was a major obstacle to her career reduced the asynchrony in her life structure by "the subordination of my 'career' to marriage. I accepted it and have been largely satisfied to be <u>useful and competent</u> even if less 'known' than capable of being."

It is apparent that these professional women faced major periods of asynchronization between family and work cycles. As a group, the women in this study had life structures characterized by atypical and erratic event sequences such as that

their marriage and fertility histories are very different from
other women of their generation. Similarly, their work histories and their career achievements exhibited little correspondence with those of a comparable cohort of male academic
social scientists. It is clear that these women in no way
had careers resembling the idealized male model in regard to
progression through the academic ranks or to institutions of
higher status. Through the analysis of their life histories,
it is apparent that these women were confronted with the task
of coordinating two mutually exclusive event cycles, work and
family, at a time when the social structure provided few alternative, approved strategies of synchronization. Consequent-
ly, their resolutions of asynchrony were highly individualized
and frequently the causal link between early life choices and
later life outcomes remains obscure. In order to determine in
a more systematic way the consequences of asynchrony between
work and family cycles as well as the causal relationship between earlier and later events in a particular temporal sequence, it would be necessary to examine the life structure of
a more generalized sample of women. Given the increased numbers of employed women in contemporary society, the life history data for a more comprehensive test of the presence and
consequences of asynchrony should presently be available.

The preceding examples illustrate the role of synchronicity in life structures, although only in terms of the coordination of work and family sequences. An unexplored aspect
of the model proposed in this paper is the relationship between cycles of life experience and psychological sequences
of development. Causal relationships between movement along
one sequence and movement along all others in a life structure are suspected, but as yet there has been no direct empirical test of the effect of timing of life events on intra-
psychic processes of development. Hogan's (25) recent work
on the ordering of life events supports Neugarten's hypothesis that "off-time" or temporally-deviant life events have
adverse consequences to the timing of later life events as
well as to the life structure as a whole. However, empirical
research is needed before precise specification of the interaction between developmental processes intrinsic to the self
and to the social structure can be accomplished.

Weingarten and Daniels' (36) study of the timing of parenthood also provides some preliminary evidence that movement along the family cycle impels movement along dimensions
of psychological development as well. Specifically, they contend that parenthood is <u>not</u> a period of "moratorium" when psychological development is in abeyance but is instead a time of
active construction of future selves by women. Daniels and

Weingarten found that even those women who bring their work cycles to a halt during parenting continue to move through psychological dimensions of development. Other evidence suggests that the relationship between life experience and psychological development may be greater than previously suspected. For example, Bielby and Siegler (41) found that recent life events appear to have a significant impact on certain social-psychological measures such as locus of control, a construct frequently assumed to be trait-like and static in nature. Therefore, at the present time, there exists no empirical proof of the relationship between the timing of life events and psychological development represented as discrete processes. In theory, such a relationship is posited and evidence of its validity is beginning to accumulate.

Conclusion

In this paper, we have presented an aggregate model of the multiple developmental processes which comprise the individual life course. Through the specification of a structure which incorporates both intra-psychic and social dimensions of development, we provide a conceptual framework for the analysis of the cumulative, multivariate processes defined by antecedent-sequelae relationships in operation throughout the life course. Although empirical research as well as innovative statistical and analytical techniques will be needed before the role of synchronicity in human development is fully understood, the model illustrated here clarifies the structure and dynamics of the individual life course.

Our point of departure for the construction of this model of the individual life course has been the evident decreased importance of chronological age as an explanatory variable in developmental research. Faced with the inadequacies of a concept defined as time since birth, developmental theory clearly requires alternative conceptualizations of time which fit our contemporary understanding of the individual life course. Because human development proceeds along many dimensions at once, our conceptualization of time must be able to account for past, present and even future times in a single life simultaneously. But capturing the complexity of time in human development is a difficult task. In a sense, the goal of the developmental researcher parallels that of the biographer. As the biographer strives to make sense of a single life, the developmental researcher strives to make collective sense out of many. In both instances, the raw material of life history data must be ordered in such a way that the dynamic evolution of the self becomes clear. Our model of the individual life course offers a method based on the concept of timing for such a systematic ordering of life history data. As Barbara Tuchman has noted, "events do not happen in categories ... they happen in sequence. When they are arranged in sequence as strictly as possible ..., cause and effect that may have been previously obscure, will often become clear, like secret ink" (42). Through its incorporation of synchronicity as a fundamental regulatory mechanism, our model of the individual life course can order the relationships among event sequences as well, thus revealing the secret ink of life span development to biographer and developmental researcher alike.

References

1. P. B. Baltes, Ed., Life-Span Development and Behavior (Academic Press, New York, 1978).
2. P. B. Baltes and S. Willis, "Toward psychological theories of aging and development," in Handbook of the Psychology of Aging, J. E. Birren and K. W. Schaie, Eds. (Van Rostrand and Reinhold Company, New York, 1977), pp. 128-154.
3. J. Mortimer and R. Simmons, "Adult Socialization," in Annual Review of Sociology, R. T. Turner, J. Coleman and R. Fox, Eds. (Annual Reviews, Palo Alto, Cal., 1978), Vol. 4, pp. 421-454.
4. W. K. Runyan, "The life course as a theoretical orientation: Sequences of person-situation interaction," Journal of Personality 46, 569-593 (1978).
5. B. L. Neugarten and G. Hagestad, "Age and the life course," in Handbook of Aging and the Social Sciences, R. H. Binstock and E. Shanas, Eds. (Van Rostrand Reinhold Company, New York, 1976), pp. 35-57.
6. K. F. Riegel, "Adult life crises: Toward a dialectical theory of development," in Life-Span Developmental Psychology: Normative Life Crises, N. Datan and L. Ginsberg, Eds. (Academic Press, New York, 1975), pp. 99-128.
7. R. N. Butler, "Toward a psychiatry of the life cycle: Implications of socio-psychological studies of the aging process for policy and practice of psychotherapy," in Aging and Modern Society: Psycho-social and Medical Aspects, A. Simon and L. J. Epstein, Eds. (American Psychiatric Association, Washington, D. C., 1968).
8. R. N. Butler and M. I. Lewis, Aging and Mental Health (C. V. Mosby, St. Louis, 1977), p. 138.
9. B. L. Neugarten, "Continuities and discontinuities of psychological issues into adult life," Human Development 12, 121-130 (1969), p. 125.
10. Ibid, p. 125.
11. B. L. Neugarten and G. Hagestad, "Age and the life course," p. 45.

12. B. L. Neugarten, "Dynamics of transition of middle age to old age," Journal of Geriatric Psychiatry 4, 71-87 (1970), pp. 86-87.
13. K. F. Riegel, "Toward a dialectical theory of development," Human Development 18, 50-64 (1975)
14. Idem, "The dialectics of human development," American Psychologist 31, 689-700 (1976).
15. Ibid., p. 695.
16. Idem, "Toward a dialectical theory," pp. 62-63.
17. D. Eichorn, "Asynchronizations in adolescent development," in Adolescence in the Life Cycle, S. E. Dragastin and G. Elder, Jr., Eds. (John Wiley and Sons, New York, 1975).
18. D. M. Baer, "An age-irrelevant concept of development," Merrill-Palmer Quarterly 16, 238-246 (1970).
19. J. Wohlwill, The Study of Behavioral Development (Academic Press, New York, 1973).
20. J. Loevinger, Ego Development (Jossey-Bass, San Francisco, 1976), pp. 32-33.
21. L. Kohlberg, "FROM IS TO OUGHT: How to commit the naturalistic fallacy and get away with it in the study of mordevelopment," in Cognitive Development and Epistemology, T. Mischel, Ed. (Academic Press, New York, 1971), p. 217.
22. J. Piaget, "Piaget's theory," in Carmichael's Manual of Child Psychology, P. H. Mussen, Ed. (John Wiley, New York, 1970).
23. L. Kohlberg, "The development of children's orientations toward a moral order: I. Sequence in the development of moral thought," Human Development 6, 11-33 (1963).
24. L. Kohlberg and R. Mayer, "Development as the aim of education," Harvard Educational Review 42, 449-496 (1978).
25. D. P. Hogan, "The variable order of events in the life course," American Sociological Review 43, 573-586 (1978).
26. M. M. Marini, "The transition to adulthood: Sex differences in educational attainment and age at marriage," American Sociological Review 43, 483-507 (1978).
27. K. F. Riegel, "Past and future trends in gerontology," Gerontologist 17, 105-113 (1977), p. 112.
28. R. L. Gould, Transformations: Growth and Change in Adult Life (Simon and Schuster, New York, 1978).
29. D. J. Levinson, The Seasons of a Man's Life (Alfred Knopf, New York, 1978.
30. P. J. Stein and H. Etzkowitz,"Life shifts in the adult life spiral: An alternative to the life cycle model," paper presented at the 73rd Annual Meeting of the American Sociological Association, San Francisco (1978).
31. G. Elder, Jr., "Adolescence in the life cycle: An introduction," in Adolescence in the Life Cycle, S. Dragastin and G. Elder, Jr., Eds. (John Wiley and Sons, New York, (1975) p. 17.

32. N. B. Tuma, M. T. Hannan and L. P. Groeneveld, "Dynamic analysis of event histories," <u>American Journal of Sociology 84</u>, 820-854 (1979).
33. P. J. Perun and D. D. V. Bielby, "Toward a model of occupational behavior: A human development approach," paper presented at the 73rd Annual Meeting of the American Sociological Association, San Francisco (1978).
34. V. K. Oppenheimer, "The life-cycle squeeze: The interaction of men's occupational and family life cycles," <u>Demography</u> 11, 227-245 (1974).
35. P. C. Glick, "The life cycle of the family," <u>Marriage and Family 17</u>, 3-9 (1955).
36. K. Weingarten and P. Daniels, "Family/career transitions in women's lives," paper presented at the American Psychological Association Symposium on Transitional Experiences in Adult Development, Toronto (1978).
37. Ibid, p. 5.
38. P. J. Perun, <u>A Study of Productivity in Academic Women Social Scientists</u>, Ph.D. dissertation, The University of Chicago, Committee on Human Development, Chicago (1977).
39. Idem, "Academic women, productivity and status attainment: A life course model," working paper, Center for Research on Women, Wellesley College, Wellesley, Mass. (1979).
40. R. J. Havighurst, "Ranking scheme of American universities and colleges," unpublished paper, The University of Chicago, Committee on Human Development, Chicago (1974).
41. D. D. V. Bielby and I. C. Siegler, "Internal-external locus of control in middle and late life: The search for construct validation," paper presented at the 30th Annual Meeting of the Gerontological Society, San Francisco (1978).
42. B. Tuchman, "Biography as a prism of history," <u>Telling Lives: The Biographer's Art</u>, M. Pachter, Ed. (New Republic Books, Washington, D. C., 1979), p. 144.

7. Terman's Gifted Women: Work and the Way They See Their Lives

In 1922, Lewis Terman began his now well-known study of gifted children (Terman, 1925). Over the years these gifted children have been tested and queried on ten occasions about almost every aspect of their lives: adjustment, ambition, health, education, occupational attainments, marital satisfaction, sources and amount of life satisfaction, political and religious views, and, of course, intelligence itself. The present paper is concerned with the women in Terman's gifted group and their subjective perceptions in 1977 of what events or choices have been important in their lives and how these things have come to be influential.

Work and Life Satisfaction of the Gifted Women in 1972

At the time of the 1972 questionnaire, the majority of the Terman group were anticipating retirement and they were in a position to review their lives' work. While they were asked about many different aspects of their lives, the findings of Sears and Barbee (1977) about women's work satisfaction in relation to other aspects of their lives are of special interest here.

The women were first classified as being "satisfied" with their work pattern -- whether it had been a career, intermittent work for income, or being a housewife -- or "not satisfied" according to the correspondence between what pattern they would now choose and what they had, in fact, lived. There were generally higher proportions of women satisfied with their work patterns among women heading households (widows, divorced women, and single women) than among married women. Within each category -- head of house or non-household head -- there were higher rates of satisfaction among women who had no children than among mothers. Women who had worked for income for at least 20

years were more often satisfied with this pattern than
homemakers were with theirs although the overall levels of
reported satisfaction with pattern chosen among all the
women was high.

Satisfaction with one's work pattern then seems to be
enhanced by having independent status (the need to support
oneself) and by being free of the role conflicts working
mothers experience -- especially those of this generation.
Work pattern satisfaction also was associated with the
level of the woman's occupation, her general life satisfaction, her health, her general adjustment and her self
described ambition for excellence.

These findings from the 1972 follow-up suggest that
work for these gifted women is associated with the
experience of independent responsibility and with her
capacity -- both physical and motivational -- for consistent
pursuit of her own plans. Here we explore further the
relationship between a woman's work history and her sources
of life satisfaction as reflected in the way she subjectively views her own life.

The Present Analysis

We asked each respondent in 1977 to identify up to five
life events which stood out as particularly significant
either because they were turning points at which choices had
to be made or because of their impact on the events that
followed. We also asked for open-ended comments on each
event in order to gather some insight into how the
respondent perceived the event to have the impact that it,
in fact, did have.

Of particular interest here is the perceptions of women
respondents concerning whether their significant life
events "happened" to them or were caused by them. Since
work in our society often requires at least some decision
making and since women, more often than men, have some
option about whether to or how much to work, I expected
that the experience of working for income would be associated with the subjective experience of "making one's life
happen" at least to some degree. Since women -- especially
in the Terman women's generation -- may experience more
ambivalence about their choices to work or not than men do,
it was of interest to look at the over-all positive or
negative effects the women perceive their life events to
have had. Also, since women with substantial work histories
have apportioned their lifetime in clearly different ways
than women with little or no work for income, it is of

interest to look at differences in the subjective content of
women's lives among groups of women whose work involvement
and/or marital statuses differ.

Let us now pursue these questions through some simple,
and yet revealing, analyses.

Method

Subjects

The Terman study staff believes the 1977 questionnaires
were received by about 650 women and of these, 374 returned
their questionnaires as of October 19, 1978. The analyses
reported here began in April of 1978 and at that time we
had 175 returned questionnaires from women who had responded
to the open-ended request to identify and comment on five
"most significant" life events. Thus this paper is
concerned with those women in the Terman sample who returned
their 1977 questionnaires by April, 1978 and who wrote at
least one significant event.

The significant life events were coded in three ways
which were of interest because of their expected relationship to women's work histories and marital statuses. First,
I simply classified the content of the events into the
various types shown in Table 1. Second, in order to study
a possible relationship between women's involvement in the
world of work outside the home and their sense of directing
their own lives, I assigned a score to each subject
representing the proportion of her significant events she
perceived as following from some decision or act of her own.
Two independent coders achieved a per-event agreement rate
of 94 percent. In later analyses, women were divided into
"internal" and "external" groups according as these
proportions were above or below the median. Finally, to
answer questions about the general emotional quality of
women's lives as they themselves see tham, I classified
each event as having a subjectively positive or negative
impact on the respondent's life and then used as a score
the proportion of reported events that were seen as
"positive." (Per-event agreement among two coders for this
aspect was 100%.) In later analyses the women are classified as primarily "positive" or primarily "negative"
according as these proportions were above and below the
median.

These two variables -- content of significant events,
internal vs. external control, and positive vs. negative
impact of events -- were the basis for a comparison among

Table 1. Categories for the Content of Significant Life Events

---

Family (marriage, children, grandchildren, parents,
 relatives)
Finances
Health
Loss (death and separation)
Mentors
Personal growth (therapy, religious experience, other
 philosophical change)
Retirement
Social and Community Involvement (offices held,
 experiences had)
Terman Study (being in it)
Vicarious Events (achievements, marriages, etc. of
 (others)
Work and Achievement (in Education, profession, or
 "other" domain)

---

women with no, some, high, and very high involvement in
work outside the home. These <u>work involvement</u> categories
were defined on the basis of a continuous work involvement
score which varied from 0 to 20 and was a function of the
number of five-year intervals (out of 10 usually) of adult
life the respondent had worked full-time (2 points) or part
time (1 point). The same three variables were also used to
compare marital status categories (married, divorced or
widowed five or more years, single). Women who had worked
some part of their lives were asked how this had affected
their marriages. The positive vs. negative aspect of these
responses was studied in relation to work involvement and
marital status.

Results

Table 1 shows the categories used to classify the content
of significant life events. The frequency with which these
categories were reported were studied in relation to
marital status and work involvement. Four categories of
work involvement (none, some, much, very much) were derived
from a continuous score which could range from 0 to 20 and
which had the means and standard deviations for marital
status groups as follows = Married, 6.01 (5.22); Widowed,
9.62 (4.95); Divorced, 11.91 (3.65); and Single 15.59 (4.70).

In general there are few relationships between work
involvement and the content of the events women see as
significant. Among Divorced and Widowed women, only one
comparison emerged as significant (Fisher exact $p < .05$)
and it was the same for both of these groups: women with
very high work involvement significantly more often reported
experiences of loss or separation than did such women with
less work involvement. Among married women, those with high
or very high work involvement significantly more often
reported loss and separation events and the experience of
educational achievements than did their counterparts with
less work involvement. Married women with some or no work
experience reported experiences of moving their homes and
of travel significantly more often than married women who
worked more.

Since a large number of analyses were made, we shall
interpret these few differences with caution. However, the
relationship between a high work involvement and the
importance of loss and/or separation, does consistently
recurr and may indicate an effect of work on what a woman
selects from her experience as significant. A related note
of interest is the finding that those women who have lost

Table 2. Work Involvement in Relation to Internal vs. External Control and Positive vs. Negative Impact

Marital Status	Married				Widowed				Divorced				Single
Work Involvement	None	Some	Much	Very Much	None	Some	Much	Very Much	None	Some	Much	Very Much	Very Much
No. of Cases	23	24	20	28	1	8	11	22	1	1	2	14	17
Proportion "Internal"	13	42	35	47	0	25	9	45	0	0	50	79	76
Proportion Positive	39	42	45	50	–	40	18	59	–	86	75	57	71

marriage through divorce or death mention it more often than married women do ($\chi2 = 5.01$, $p < .05$). A life event that was in some sense "at issue" is seen as significant. A similar theme is illustrated by the finding that married women and widows (who were married for many years) mention achievements more often than single and divorced women ($\chi2 = 8.92$, $p < .05$).

Divorced women include "personal growth" and other people's experiences significantly less often than do other women ($\chi2 = 7.56$ and 17.44, $p < .01$). These women have been forced into focusing on their own growth and into being less dependent on other people's lives to give significance to their own. These matters are not "at issue" for divorcees and thus less frequently are listed as significant.

Table 2 presents the relationship between women's being (or not being) primarily "internal" in her recollection of life events and their degree of involvement in work.

Chi Square analyses for each marital status except single indicate that women who have worked more are more likely to be classified as "internal" than women who have worked less (χ's = 13.00, 5.03, 8.56, $p < .05$). Women substantially involved in work see their lives as having followed from their own decisions and acts whereas women who have been little or not at all involved in work see their lives as having evolved through events outside their own control. Indeed, Married women with very much work involvement do not differ from single women in their internality.

Analyses of the marital status groups showed that the combined married and widowed group was less internally oriented that the divorced and single women ($\chi2 = 32.21$, $p < .001$). Overall, satisfactory marriage is associated more often with a subjective view of life as happening whereas the single or single-again status is associated more often with a sense of making life happen.

Table 2 also shows that the overal proportion of Terman women who see their life events having primarily positive impact is high. There is essentially no relationship between work involvement and this proportion within any marital status group and there are also no significant differences among the marital status groups. It is possible that the overall high level of "positiveness" may here as elsewhere (Campbell, Converse & Rodgers, 1976) obscure any relationship that does exist.

The question about the impact of work on marriage may have had quite different effects on respondents currently married than it had on divorcees and widows whose answers were based on memories varying greatly in age. Formal analysis was attempted only for women still married. They reported essentially three kinds of effects: improvement in financial status, improvement of the emotional climate within the marriage, and reduction in discretionary time available to the couple. Work involvement was related to only one of these perceived effects: Married women with the highest degree of work involvement reported improved emotional climate in marriage significantly more often than other married women ($\chi 2$ = 5.19, p .05).

Discussion

As the Terman gifted women reflect back over the courses of their lives they identify significant events that show a remarkable commonality among women in the group: education, marriage, family, and personal achievements turn up on almost all the lists. However, despite this commonality of what life's content has been, women who have worked more see this content differently than women who have worked less do. Those who have worked for most of their adult lives view their lives as something they have created whereas women who have seldom worked see their lives as having evolved largely outside of their own control.

The relationship between work and the internally oriented perception of one's life may arise in one of three ways. Straightforwardly, the Terman women tend to have work that (while not as highly prestigious as those of the Terman men) required some responsibility . . . and required them to make at least some decisions. Over a lifetime, these work experiences may have become "habits of mind" in which the women's reflections about their lives tended to be expressed in terms of activities and choices of their own. An also straightforward, but alternative possibility is the one that women's cognitive characteristics have determined their behavior. In this instance, the argument would be that the same ones that correlated with educational and occupational achievement -- also oriented them towards seeing their lives as being under their own control. Indeed, there is evidence that training, education, and experience with achievement do have precisely these kinds of effects (Lefcourt, 1976).

While we have not yet searched our archives for predictors of the gifted women's internal vs. external control status, previous work with the sample, and research with the internal-external control dimension suggest some hypotheses: the groups of women who were high occupational achievers in 1960 and who were most satisfied with their work status in 1972 tended to include a higher proportion of single women, childless married women, or mothers of only children than did the group as a whole (Oden, 1968; Sears and Barbee, 1977.) Here we see that the fewer sources of intimate external control a gifted woman has, the more achieving, in fact, and satisfied with an achieving life pattern she may be. The women who work most in each marital status group in 1977 may be those least influenced by such sources of intimate external control -- either because such sources are absent literally or because the husbands and children who are present do not exert much "external" control on the women (at least to perform traditional domestic roles). Thus, the single, divorced, and working married women's tendency toward "internality" may result from the absence of pressures to suppress it commonly exerted on other women in society (Lefcourt, 1976).

An alternative possibility for the higher internality scores among married working women relative to married homemakers: It may be that they were exposed to pressures towards traditional role involvement but resisted such influences because of their internal orientations. Such resistance to influence is known to characterize people with high internality scores on conventional paper and pencil measures (Lefcourt, 1976).

A third set of possibilities for the source of the work-and-internality association involves some of the actions of so-called "third variables." Some of the gifted women may have been impelled both to work much and to see their lives internally as a consequence of their life experiences with independence training, exposure to "internal" models, and encouragement to achieve. These possibilities need to be explored.

The marital status of the Terman women was a predictor of their internal vs. external control status. Married and widowed women are relatively more "external" in their discriptions of their lives while divorced and single women are relatively more "internal." While numbers become quite small for statistical analysis, it is apparent from perusal of Table 2 that this apparent "marital status effect" arises out of the different work involvement levels of these two groups of women.

Work, then, is a significant predictor of how a Terman gifted woman perceives the events of her life: whether she sees them as arising more out of her own choices and committments or from the choices and committments of others. These women are clearly emotionally involved in the traditional "women's worlds" of their families, homes, and communities as seen in the contents of their lives as they describe them. The differences among the women arise not in the realm of <u>what</u> is important but in the manner whereby important things are seen to have their influence. The family centered, and yet independent, "external," Terman gifted woman in her 60s may be the foremother of the woman of more typical intelligence in the 1970s who is coming to see herself as mistress of her own destiny, albeit the one with room for relationships, community, and, often, family.

Most of the women saw their lives in terms of events that had had generally positive effects on them. The large proportion of positive life events corresponds with other studies of life satisfaction such as the Campbell survey which asked respondents how "happy" they felt (Campbell, Converse, Rodgers, 1976). Nevertheless, it is of interest to see this same pattern reflected in lists and coding of significant events as in the more direct questioning about happiness. It may be that the gifted women -- like others -- prefer to report positive things. Alternatively, perhaps we all tend to actually remember the good things better than the bad. Perhaps something more dynamic goes on: As the years go by we may come to a greater perspective on the events which have made up our lives; we may see the good and the bad but tend to conceptualize the impact of events more in terms of the impetus to make us do or decide things that ultimately, if not immediately, were good for us. Indeed comments to this effect were frequently made by the Terman women, who would write something like "Initially my father's death was devastating, but I realized I had to stand on my own," or, "My family's move to Grand Rapids frightened me, but I made new friends and the confidence I gained has helped me fight life's battles." or, "The loss of our daughter was over-whelming . . . but eventually it brought us to a realization of how much we need each other.

Most women in the group, then, agreed about what has emerged as important in life and that, overall, life has been very satisfying. There were a few differences, and while these were minor, they suggested an interesting pattern. Experiences of loss and achievement through work were made most often by still-married or widowed women

rather than by single or long-divorced women. Marriage is
more often listed by women who have lost it through divorce
or death than by those who still have it. Divorced women
stand out in that they report no experiences of other
people as significant events in their own lives and they
also report no personal growth (therapy, significant
religious experience, new insights). Events that are in
some sense problematic or "at issue" seem to be reported
disproportionately often. Marriage has been placed at
issue for widows and divorcees whereas the opportunity to
achieve in work has been an issue for married women. The
experience of loss may be more memorable to a working woman
who has conflicts about her work and her relationships.
Finally a woman who has been divorced necessarily has to
grow and change and rely more on herself than on others
in her life after divorce. Thus, these things are non-
issues to her and are therefore not reported as significant.

As a whole these findings show the experience of work
has had a positive impact on those Terman women who have
had it. They are as positive about their lives as other
Terman women and their marriages and family lives have the
same importance to them as they do to the women who worked
little or not at all. The working Terman woman has come to
experience her life as a creation of her own and, if
married, she sees this creation as having improved the
marriage.

These gifted women are from a generation for whom a
woman's working outside the home was definitely not the
expected pattern. Many of them nevertheless worked for
substantial portions of their lives though often at
traditionally feminine occupations (education, librarianship,
nursing). There is certainly no evidence that this work
provided any clear routes to superior lives or greater
happiness, it is evident that this work did not damage a
woman's chances for great satisfaction in life, successful
marriage, or the joy of family life. What the work
experience may have done for these women is enable them to
look back over their lives with a greater subjective sense
of accomplishment than they would otherwise experience.
Today's highly intelligent and educated working woman may
expect more from lifetime of work effort and therefore she
may not in the future view her life as positively as the
Terman working women unless her expectations are fulfilled.
Since all young women today have a greater sense of choice
than women of the Terman group's generation, internality
may not remain the province of the working woman. What the
Terman women's gifts may have provided them is a capacity
for experiencing accomplishment and satisfaction in the

choices which they could and did make and the ability to
resist the lessening of self-esteem that less gifted
working women of their age may have endured when they chose
non-traditional life styles.

References

Campbell, A., Converse, P.E., & Rodgers, W.L. The Quality
   of American Life. New York: Russell-Sage, 1976.

Lefcourt, H.M. Locus of Control. Hillsdale, N.J.: Erlbaum,
   1976.

Oden, M.H. Fulfillment of Promise: Forty-Year Follow-up
   of the Terman Gifted Group. Genetic Psychology
   Monographs, 1968, 77, 3-93.

Sears, P.S. & **Barbee,** A. Career and Life Satisfaction Among
   Terman's Gifted Women. Dr. J. Stanley, W.C. Geroge, &
   C.H. Solano (Eds.) The Gifted and the Creative: A Fifty
   Year Perspective. Baltimore: John Hopkins University
   Press, 1977.

Terman, L.M. Genetic Studies of Genius: I. Mental and
   Physical Traits of a Thousand Gifted Children. Stanford,
   Calif.: Stanford University Press, 1925.

Barbara Myerhoff

8. Life History Among the Elderly: Performance, Visibility and Re-Membering

Abstract

Life Histories are regarded as both process and
product, especially useful in establishing a self-
definition and providing visibility. A group of old
people is described here, engaged in collective self-
definition ("Definitional Ceremonies") and personal
but publicly-presented and performed Life History
work ("Living History Classes"). Several factors
are cited that make this an important pursuit for
them: the absence of natural audiences and rupture
in inter-generational continuity; the destruction of
their natal culture; and the trivialization and
neglect of the elderly routinely practiced in contemporary American society. Witnessing themselves
as heroes in their own dramas of existence, and
vividly, publicly remembering their shared past makes
the group both potent and acutely self-conscious.
Their attainment of integration is viewed as an
essential task for the last part of the life cycle.

Part of the funding for the research on which this paper is
based was provided by the National Science Foundation, through
the Andrus Gerontology Center of the University of Southern
California, in connection with a study of "Ethnicity and
Aging." The author's book <u>Number Our Days</u>, E. P. Dutton,
1979, presents a fuller treatment of the subject. All materials quoted from the elderly subjects come from that source.
All names of individuals and organizations have been changed.

Slowly it comes out from them
their beginning to their ending,
slowly you can see it in them the
nature and the mixtures in them,
slowly everything comes out from
each one in the kind of repeating
each one does in the different
parts and kinds of living they have
in them, slowly then the history of
them comes out from them, slowly then
any one who looks well at any one
will have the history of the whole
of that one. Slowly the history
of each one comes out of each one.

Gertrude Stein
Lectures in America

Karl Mannheim observed that "Individuals who belong to
the same generation, who share the same year of birth, are
endowed, to that extent, with a common location in the historical dimension of the social process."(1) Often, however,
membership in a common cohort is background information, like
grammatical rules, more interesting to outside analysts than
members. Outsiders find and want explanations where the subjects continue unself-consciously in the habits of everyday
life. Sometimes conditions conspire that make a generational
cohort acutely self-conscious and then they become active participants in their own history, and provide their own sharp,
insistent definitions of themselves and explanations for their
destiny, past and future. They are then knowing actors in a
historical drama which they script, rather than subjects in
someone else's study. They "make" themselves, sometimes even
"make themselves up," an activity which is not inevitable or
automatic but reserved for special people and special circumstances. It is an artificial and exhilarating undertaking,
this self-construction. As with all conspicuously made-up
ventures (rituals are perhaps the best example), acute self-
consciousness may become destructive, paralyzing actors in a
spasm of embarrassed lack of conviction. But occasionally
self-consciousness does not interfere with personal and cultural construction; rather it provides another, fuller angle
of self-understanding. Then the subjects know that their
knowing is a component of their conduct. They assume responsibility for inventing themselves and yet maintain their sense
of authenticity and integrity. Such people exercise power
over their images, in their own eyes and to some extent in the
eyes of whoever may be observing them. Sometimes the image is
the only part of their lives subject to control. But this is
not a small thing to control. It may lead to a realization of

personal power, and serve as a source of pleasure and understanding in the workings of consciousness. Heightened self-
consciousness -- self-awareness -- is not an essential, omnipresent attainment. It does not always come with age, and is
probably not critical to well-being. But when it does occur,
it may bring one into a greater fullness of being; one may
become a more fully realized example of the possibilities of
being human. This is not small compensation in extreme old
age.

    The group described here is such an acutely self-
conscious one, making itself up, knowing that this is going on,
doing it well and appreciating the process. This is a subtle
but distinctive state of consciousness, revealed in their personal and collective concerns. Many factors enhance this
self-consciousness, not the least of which is their sense of
bearing what Tamara Hareven calls "generational memories."
She uses this term to refer to "the memories which individuals have of their own families' history, as well as more generational collective memories about their past."(2) The subjects of this paper are heirs to a set of memories of a culture and society extinguished during the Holocaust. Very old
and close to death, they realize that there will be no others
after them with direct-experience of their natal culture. And
because inter-generational continuity has not been sustained,
there are no clear heirs to their memories. The old peoples'
sense of being memory bearers, carriers of a precious, unique
cargo, heightens generational memory and intensifies cohort-
consciousness, giving a mission to the group that is at once
urgent and at the same time unlikely to be realized. Their
machinations to accomplish their task, delivering themselves
of their memories, establishing, then making visible their own
identities, illuminates several matters: the nature of performed individual and collective definitions, the uses and
kinds of witnesses needed for these performances and the nature and uses of memory. Life histories are seen here as giving opportunities to allow people to become visible, and to
enhance reflexive consciousness. For the very old, in this
population in particular, this may be construed as work essential to the last stage in the life cycle.

Ethnographic Setting

    In 1972 I began an investigation of a group of elderly
Jews, immigrants from Eastern Europe, who had lived on their
own in an open setting for many years, often two to three
decades. During this time they had developed a singularly
rich and strong subculture, drawing on their common religious
and ethnic past, derived from their lives as children in the
shtetls and towns whose culture centered around the Yiddish

language and the folk tradition known as <u>Yiddishkeit</u>.   The
childhood layer of history was augmented by that of their
middle years in the New World, when they worked as unskilled
laborers for the most part, toward the goal of giving their
children economic advantages, education, and all that was
necessary to assure their successful and swift assimilation
into American society.   The old people retained from this
period their patriotism for America and identification with
such values as freedom, democracy and egalitarianism.   Most
discarded the religious orthodoxy of their parents when they
immigrated at the turn of the century, but though often ag-
nostics or atheists, they were strongly identified with cultural or ethnic Judaism.   Zionism was a common bond among
them, as was Yiddishkeit, and the social-political values expressed by their work as Internationalists, Bundists, Social-
ists and trade unionists.   These ingredients and experiences
were woven together into a motley but sturdy set of practices
and ideas adapted to their contemporary circumstances.

These circumstances were harsh.   Most of the 4,000 individuals identified by these characteristics lived along the
beach front in a transitional and dangerous neighborhood.
Nearly all were poor, living on fixed incomes in small rented
rooms or apartments, inadequate and overpriced.   Transporta-
tion in and out of the area was also inadequate.   Relatives
were distant and dispersed.   Children -- culturally as well
as geographically distant -- rarely visited them.   Their con-
tacts with all outsiders were attenuated and ceremonial, not
a steady part of their everyday life.   Few Jewish organizations or individuals gave them much attention or aid; their
isolation was extreme.   Now in their 80's and 90's, most were
frail, often ill but fiercely independent, determined to care
for themselves and preserve their autonomy.

Paradoxically the isolation of the old people contributed
to the vigor of their improvised subculture.   Having been left
alone, they were forced to turn to each other for company and
abide the considerable ideological differences among them.
And with no children around to embarrass with their "green-
horn" ways, they freely revitalized those parts of their tradition that they enjoyed and found valuable, while sloughing
off those American customs that did not appeal to them.

The people were bearers of a culture that would die with
them, and this was well-known to all.   They were an invisible
people, marginal to mainstream American society, an impotent
group -- economically, physically, and politically. This they
fought off as well as they could, as relentlessly they struggled to maintain their place in their own community, and when
possible, to find a moment's attention from the larger outside

world. They knew they were irreplaceable and their consciousness of being the people who remembered a culture destroyed
by the Holocaust fed their determination not to be extinguished until the last possible moment. Nevertheless, they knew
they would lose in this struggle. Death, impotence, invisi-
bility were omnipresent threats. But the atmosphere in the
community was not one of defeat or despair. On the contrary,
in it there was intensity and vitality, humor, irony and dignity. Always the people exuded a sense of living meaningful
lives. Despite the evidence of their insignificance offered
by the outside world, they were quite clear about their own
importance. It is my interpretation that their self-
consciousness, promoted by collective performances and private
self-narration, their recounting of stories and life histories,
influenced and nourished their success as old people.

The focus of the social life of this assembly was a secular Senior Citizen Center -- the Aliyah Center -- funded and
sponsored by a larger umbrella Jewish organization. Official-
ly 250 to 400 people were members but many more used the Center than joined. This use was intense and the concept of
"voluntary organization" disguises the amount of time and the
importance of the Center to its constituents. The programs
and services it offered made it possible for many to remain
living in an open setting. Daily inexpensive hot meals were
available. Social services, ceremonies -- secular and religious -- celebrations of life crises, classes, and recreation
occurred there. Members were a genuine primary group, despite
the frequent ruptures and factions among them. The boardwalk
which the Center faced was an outdoor extension, almost a
village plaza, in which socializing continued before the Center opened and after it closed.

I came to the Center in 1972, to examine ethnicity and
aging, as part of a larger study of aging in various cultures,
and remained to work there for two years on a full-time basis,
and less intensively ever since.

Self-Presentation and Performing: Becoming Visible

Cultures include in their work self-presentations to
their members. On certain collection occasions, cultures offer interpretations. They tell stories, comment, portray and
mirror. Like all mirrors, cultures are not accurate reflec-
tors; there are distortions, contradictions, reversals, exag-
gerations and even lies. Nevertheless, self-knowledge, for
the individual and collectivity, is the consequence. These
portraits range from delicate and oblique allusions through
fully staged dramatic productions in the course of which members embody their place in the scheme of things, their locations

in the social structure, their purposes and natures, taking up
the questions of who we are and why we are here which as a
species we cannot do without. Such performances are opportunities for appearing, an indispensable ingredient of being
itself, for unless we exist in the eyes of others we may come
to doubt even our own existence. Being is a social, psychological construct, made not given. Thus it is erroneous to
think of performances as optional, arbitrary, or merely deco-
rative embellishments as we in Western societies are inclined
to do. In this sense, arenas for appearing are essential and
culture serves as a stage as well as mirror providing opportunities for self- and collective proclamations of being.

Since these constructions are intentionally designed they
are not only reflections of "what is"; they are also opportunities to write history as it should be or should have been,
demonstrating a culture's notion of propriety and sense. History and accident are not permitted to be imposed willy-nilly,
those badly written, haphazard, incomplete recordings of occurrences that are so unsatisfactory. Rather performances are
shaped and groomed justifications, more akin to myth and religion than lists of empty external events we call history or
chronicle.(3)

The performative dimension of culture seen most often in
rituals, ceremonies, festivals, celebrations and the like are
properly understood as both instrumental and expressive. They
blur our overstated dichotomies between art and science, myth
and reality, religion and work, subjective and objective.

The central challenge to such performances is that of
conviction. They must play well and persuade players and audiences that what is seen is what is. The virtual magic of
"once upon a time," the "willing suspension of disbelief,"
"the fusion of the lived-in and dreamed-of orders" -- these
are some of the ways we speak about the capacity to arouse
conviction through performance.(4) Because of the active dimension implicit in these forms, persuasion is achieved less
by cognition than emotion and physiology. The extreme employment of the senses in these moments convinces the body, and
the mind follows. "Doing is believing" in such cases and
'sensory' as opposed to what Langer calls 'discursive' symbols
are used, because of their extraordinary capacity to make the .
improbable momentarily beyond question.(5)

When such performances are successful, we receive experience rather than belief. Then the invisible world is made
manifest, whether this is a prosaic affair such as demonstrating the fact of a rearranged social relationship, or a grander
more mysterious presentation involving supernatural beings or

principles. In all events the performed order is explicit, realized, and we are <u>within</u> it, not only left to endlessly wonder or talk about it.(6) Any reality is capable of being made convincing if it combines art, knowledge, authentic symbols and rituals, and is validated by appropriate witnesses.

Cultural performances are reflective in the sense of showing ourselves to ourselves. They are also capable of being reflexive, arousing consciousness of ourselves as we see ourselves. As heroes in our own dramas, we are made self-aware, conscious of our consciousness. At once actor and audience, we may then come into the fullness of our human capability -- and perhaps human desire -- to watch ourselves and enjoy knowing that we know. All this requires skill, craft, a coherent, consensually validated set of symbols and social arenas for appearing. It also requires an audience in addition to performers. When cultures are fragmented and in serious disarray, proper audiences may be hard to find. Natural occasions may not be offered and then they must be artificially invented. I have called such performances "Definitional Ceremonies," understanding them to be collective self-definitions specifically intended to proclaim an interpretation to an audience not otherwise available.(7) The latter must be captured by any means necessary and made to see the truth of the group's history as the members understand it. Socially marginal people, disdained, ignored groups, individuals with what Erving Goffman calls "spoiled identities," regularly seek opportunities to appear before others in the light of their own internally provided interpretation.

Among the Center members Definitional Ceremonies were a major part of their collective behavior. Again and again, they attempted to show outsiders, as well as each other, who they were, why they mattered, what the nature of their past and present lives were. Many circumstances contributed to the urgency with which they engaged in this activity. Their extreme old age and sense of little time remaining intensified the desire to formulate a presentation of themselves. Added to this was their anguish due to acute neglect. The outside world had turned its eyes away. And their very bodies had abandoned them in terms of providing evidence of their continuing clear existence. Senses and appetite had dimmed. Wakefulness often merged into dozing. Memory was quixotic and cognitive control irregular. Physical contact with others was sharply limited since by cultural custom they rarely touched each other save for an occasional ceremonial embrace or when dancing. Sensory deprivation contributed to the blunting of a sharp sense of self and being. Others were needed to affirm not only that their lives mattered but that they were really there at all. This was made hideously plain not long ago when

a bicyclist on the boardwalk struck and killed one of the old
women. He said, "I didn't see her," though onlookers agreed
she had been standing directly before him and he seemed to be
looking directly at her. It was as though she was not a real
presence.

Attention was the scarce goods in the community. Everyone competed for it with astonishing fierceness. The sight of
a camera or tape recorder, the mere possibility that someone
would sit down and listen to them, aroused the members' appetite to have themselves documented. One of the members was
heartbroken when she was not elected to the Board of Directors.
"How will anyone know I am here?" she asked. If possible, the
attention should come from outsiders who were more socially
prestigious and therefore more capable of certifying their
existence. And if possible, these should be younger people,
because peers would soon be gone. Who then would be left to
recall their existence? What Sir Thomas Browne said in 1658
is still true. The threat of oblivion is "the heaviest stone
that melancholy can throw at a man."

Performance is not merely a vehicle for being seen. Self-
definition is attained through it and this is tantamount to
being what one claims to be. "We become what we display,"
says Mircea Eliade in discussing the transformative power of
ritual performances. The imposition of meaning occurs when
we select from the myriad possibilities a particular formulation that summarizes and epitomizes. Enactments are inten-
tional, not spontaneous, rhetorical and didactic, taming the
chaos of the world, at once asserting existence and meaning.

Meaning and 'Re-Membering'

The necessity for meaning is probably ubiquitous. In the
Center population it was elevated to a passion. The old people were inclined naturally toward self-consciousness by their
tradition's emphasis on their unique status as a Chosen People.
The historical facts of their lives since the Dispersion from
the Holy Land exacerbated this tendency since Jews have spent
so much of their history as pariah peoples surrounded by hos-
tile outsiders. The Holocaust further intensified their
awareness of their distinctiveness and promoted among survivors a search through the events of their private and collective lives for an explanation of their destiny. Lifton has
suggested that survivors of mass destruction often become
"seekers after justice." They carefully examine events for
evidence of something aside from chaos to account for their
sufferings. Indications of a moral and sane universe become
imperative to ward off despair. Sense must be resurrected by
means of an explanation. Any disaster becomes more bearable

once it is named and conceptualized, once support is found
for the belief in the "relatively modest assertion that God
is not mad," to paraphrase Bertrand Russell's minimum definition of religion. Lifton speaks of survivors of the Holocaust
and of Hiroshima as restoring sanity to themselves through
"the formulative effort. Any experience of survival -- whether
of large disaster or intimate personal loss...involves a jour-
ney to the edge of the world of the living. The formulative
effort, the search for signs of meaning, is the survivor's
means of return from that edge."(8)

The survivors of catastrophe, like the victims of disaster, must account for their escape. Job-like, victims peti-
tion the gods to know their sins, asking for explanations as
to why they deserved their fate. But we often overlook the
fact that those who are not afflicted when all around them are
also ask the gods, "Why me?" The sorting through collective
and private histories for answers was among some Center old
people nearly an obsession, and often exceedingly painful.
But the members were committed to it nonetheless. "The one
who studies history loses an eye," said Moshe. "The one who
does not loses two eyes." More formally Wilhelm Dilthey says,
"Both our fortunes and our own nature cause us pain, and so
they force us to come to terms with them through understanding. The past mysteriously invites us to know the closely-
woven meaning of its moments."(9)

Surviving and Survivor's Guilt, then, can serve as transformative agents, taking the base materials of ordinary existence and disaster and working the alchemical miracle upon
them until they result in consciousness. The consequence is
a development of the capacity to lead an examined life. This
includes the construction of an explicable, even moral universe despite crushing external evidence to the contrary. The
Center members had achieved this, and their use of rituals
and ceremonies to enliven and interpret daily life was remarkable. Every day, even every minute, was focussed in the
light of all that had been extinguished and lost. "If we
lose ourselves now, if we give up our traditions, if we become like everyone else, then we finish ourselves off. We
finish Hitler's work for him," said one of the old women.
They felt that they owed living fully to their beloved --
always the "best of us" -- who had perished. Thus were despair and depression held at bay. The old people also felt a
certain sense of triumph at having persisted despite the attempts of so many to extinguish them. Outliving their enemies
was a personal accomplishment for which they took responsibility and in which they took pride, flavored often as not by
bitterness.

Overcoming physical handicaps and poverty were also moral
accomplishments. The ability to remain independent and take
care of themselves was closely attended and valued collective-
ly by the elders. Senility and loss of autonomy were more
feared than death. Their accomplishments were finely cali-
brated, nearly inconspicuous to younger, healthy outsiders.
Basha succinctly stated her sense of achievement, even power,
when she said:

> Every morning I wake up in pain. I wiggle my toes.
> Good. They still obey. I open my eyes. Good. I
> can still see. Everything hurts but I get dressed.
> I walk down to the ocean. Good. It's still there.
> Now my day can start. About tomorrow I never know.
> After all, I'm eighty-nine. I can't live forever.

Center members' attitudes toward time were colored by
extreme age, the closeness of death, their sense of accomplishment at outliving catastrophe, and an often righteous
determination to be themselves. They were alone and angry at
being alone. They were no longer willing to trouble themselves to please others, or pretend to be what they were not.
Decorum, grace and courtesy were not for them. Truth was
permitted to this stage of life and as someone put it, "We are
just like we've always been, only more so." Time was an issue
that flickered in and out of discussions often. On one hand,
the elders felt they had plenty of it, due to their enforced
leisure. But on the other, every remaining day counted. This
was illustrated by an exchange between some of the members
discussing the existence of God.

> Nathan: If we start to talk about God now we'll
> be here for five thousand years. These questions
> you could keep for posterity.

> Sonya: Have you got better to do with your time
> than sit here and talk?

Sadie interrupted and began to talk about her ailments...
"Even the doctors don't know how I survive. I could list for
you all my sicknesses." Nathan retorted: "For this we don't
have enough time."

Yet, one of the Center's leaders, a man of ninety-five,
often wrote essays on the proper way to age and use time. His
writings included a piece called "Ten Commandments for the
Elderly." Gentle irony and a delicate sense of the precious-
ness of time remaining are apparent. No future exists so time
should be neither rushed nor rigidly saved -- the sense is
there of fully using what is left but not expecting or

demanding more.

> Dress neatly and don't try to save your best
> clothes, because after you leave this world you
> won't need them anymore. Keep your head up, walk
> straight, and don't act older than your age.
> Remember one thing: If you don't feel well, there
> are many people who are feeling worse. Walk care-
> fully, watching for the green light when crossing.
> If you have to wait a minute or two, it doesn't
> make any difference at your age. There is no
> reason to rush.

Time is abolished not only by myth and dream but occasionally also by memory, for remembering the past fully and
well retains it. Life experiences are not swept away as if
they had never been. They are rewoven into the present.
Memory was problematic very often and forgetfulness experienced as very painful. Forgetting a person, an incident,
even a word was often a torment. Shmuel explained the seri-
ousness of this. "You understand, one word is not like another...So when just the word I want hides from me, when before it has always come along very politely when I called it,
this is a special torture designed for old Jews."

Memory is a continuum ranging from vague, dim shadows to
the most bright vivid totality. At its most extreme form,
memory may offer the opportunity not merely to recall the past
but to relive it, in all its original freshness, unaltered by
intervening change and reflection. All the accompanying sen-
sations, emotions and associations of the first occurrence
are recovered and the past recaptured. Marcel Proust more
than anyone analyzed how this process works and how exceedingly precious such moments are. The process does not involve
will, volition or the conscious, critical mind. It cannot be
forced. Such moments are gifts, numinous pinpoints of great
intensity. Mendilow calls them a "kind of hermetical magic
...when one is sealed outside of time. The sense of duration
is suspended and all of life is experienced as a single moment
......concentrations of universal awareness, antithetical to
the diffuseness of life."(10) Then one's self and one's memories are experienced as eternally valid. Simultaneity re-
places sequence, and a sense of oneness with all that has
been one's history is achieved.

These moments very often involve childhood memories, and
then one may experience the self as it was originally and
know beyond doubt that one is the same person as that child,
still dwelling within a much-altered body. The integration
with earlier states of being surely provides the sense of

continuity and completeness that may be counted as essential developmental task in old age. It may not yield wisdom, the developmental task that Erikson points to as the work of this stage of life.(11)   It does give what he would consider ego integrity, the opposite of disintegration.

Freud suggests that the completion of the mourning process requires that those left behind develop a new reality which no longer includes what has been lost.(12)   But judging from the Center members' struggle to retain the past, it must be added that full recovery from mourning may restore what has been lost, maintaining it through incorporation into the present.   Full recollection and retention may be as vital to recovery and well-being as forfeiting memories.

Moments of full recollection are often triggered by sensory events -- taste, touch, smell. Often physical movements, gestures, and actions -- singing, dancing, participation in rituals, prayers, and ceremonies rooted in the archaic past -- are also triggers. Actors in the method school use these devices to re-arouse emotions, speaking of this as 'kinesthetic memory'. The body retains the experiences that may be yielded, eventually and indirectly, to the mind. Often among Center members it was possible to see this at work. In the midst of a song, a lullaby that had been sung to the old person as a child, a dance that seemed to dance the dancer, produced changes in posture, a fluidity of movement or sharply altered countenance in which youthfulness was mysteriously but undeniably apparent. And Center members were articulate about these experiences. One woman described her recovery of herself as a child, with her mother's hands on her unwrinkled face when she blessed the candles, as she had done with her mother decades before. When reciting the ancient prayer for the dead, one old man brought back the entire experience of the original context in which he first heard the prayer. Once more he felt himself a small boy standing close to his father, wrapped snugly in the father's prayer shawl, close against the cold of the bright winter morning, weeping, swaying over an open grave.

To signify this special type of recollection, the term "Re-membering" may be used, calling attention to the re-aggregation of members, the figures who belong to one's life story, one's own prior selves, as well as significant others who are part of the story. Re-membering, then, is a purposive, significant unification, quite different from the passive, continuous fragmentary flickerings of images and feelings that accompany other activities in the normal flow of consciousness. The focussed unification provided by Re-membering is requisite to sense and ordering. A life is given a

shape that extends back in the past and forward into the future. It becomes a tidy edited tale. Completeness is sac-
rificed for moral and aesthetic purposes. Here history may
approach art and ritual. The same impulse for order informs
them all. Perhaps this is why Mnemosne, the goddess of Memory among the Greeks, is the mother of the muses. Without
Re-membering we lose our histories, and our selves. Time is
erosion then rather than accumulation. Says Nabokov in his
autobiography, "...the beginning of reflexive consciousness
in the brain of our remotest ancestor must surely have coin-
cided with the dawning of the sense of time."(13)

The process is the same when done in individual lives or
by a culture or a generational cohort. Private and collective lives, properly Re-membered, are interpretative. Full or
"thick description" is such an analysis. This involves finding linkages between the group's shared, valued beliefs and
symbols, and specific historical events. Particularities are
subsumed and equated with grander themes, seen as exemplify-
ing ultimate concerns. Then such stories may be enlarged to
the level of myth as well as art -- sacred and eternal justifications for how things are and what has happened. A life,
then, is not envisioned as belonging only to the individual
who has lived it but it is regarded belonging to the World,
to Progeny who are heirs to the embodied traditions, or to
God. Such Re-membered lives are moral documents and their
function is salvific, inevitably implying, "All this has not
been for nothing."

The extraordinary struggle of Survivors to recount their
histories is explicable in this light. Again and again concentration camp literature describes inmates' determination
to come back and tell the living their stories. This is seldom with the expectation of bringing about reform or repent-
ance. It is to forge a link with the listener, to retain
one's past, to find evidence of sense -- above all it is an
assertion of an unextinguished presence. The redemption provided by Re-membering is well-understood by the storyteller
Elie Wiesel who struggled back from hell to recount the voy-
age. In the dedication of his book on Hasidism he says:

My father, an enlightened spirit, believed in man.
My grandfather, a fervent Hasid, believed in God.
The one taught me to speak, the other to sing.
Both loved stories.
And when I tell mine, I hear their voices.
Whispering from beyond the silenced storm.
They are what links the survivor to their memory.(14)

A young actress, Leeny Sack, working with the histories

of her parents as concentration camp survivors has recently
developed a theater piece. The recurrent phrase that punctu-
ates her narrative begins, "My father told me to tell you
this..." The substance was unbearable but she explained the
only pain worse than recollection was the pain of considering
the possibility that the stories would be untold.(15) His
anguish, we may assume was assuaged, by capturing his daughter as audience and giving her the task of transmitting his
account. The usual feelings aroused in the teller are grati-
tude and relief.

   A student working with one of the Center members noted
this when she completed a series of life history sessions with
one of the old women. The old woman was illiterate and completely alone. She never envisioned an opportunity to find a
proper listener. When the project was complete, the younger
woman thanked the older profoundly, having been exceptionally
moved by the older woman's strength, the range of her struggles, her determination to rise to the challenges of her life.
The older woman declined the thanks saying, "No, it is I who
thank you. Every night before I fall asleep here on my narrow bed, I go over my life. I memorize it, in case anyone
should ask."

   The prospect of death was often less fearsome than that
of dying without having had an opportunity to unburden themselves of their memories, among many of these elderly. Their
stories did not have to be complete or accurate. They realized that younger listeners who could pass them on would not
be capable of comprehending what he or she had not lived
through. But the mere remembering that there had been a history, a people, a culture, a story, would suffice. Charac-
teristically, Shmuel made this point by telling a story. He
recounted a parable concerning the founder of Hasidism, the
Baal Shem Tov.

> When the great Hasid, Baal Shem Tov, the Master of
> the Good Name, had a problem, it was his custom to
> go to a certain part of the forest. There he would
> light a fire and say a certain prayer, and find wis-
> dom. A generation later, a son of one of his disci-
> ples was in the same position. He went to that same
> place in the forest and lit the fire but he could
> not remember the prayer. But he asked for wisdom
> and it was sufficient. He found what he needed. A
> generation after that, his son had a problem like
> the others. He also went to the forest, but he
> could not even light the fire. 'Lord of the Uni-
> verse,' he prayed, 'I could not remember the prayer
> and I cannot get the fire started. But I am in the

forest. That will have to be sufficient.' And
it was.

Now, Rabbi Ben Levi sits in his study with his
head in his hands. 'Lord of the Universe,' he
prays, 'look at us now. We have forgotten the
prayer. The fire is out. We can't find our way
back to the place in the forest. We can only
remember that there was a fire, a prayer, a place
in the forest. So, Lord, now that must be sufficient.'

Upon completing a recording of his life history, Shmuel
reflected on what it meant for him to face his death knowing
his recollections of an entire way of life would be lost. His
town in Poland that he had loved in his childhood no longer
existed, destroyed in the Holocaust.

...it is not the worst thing that can happen for
a man to grow old and die. But here is the hard
part. When my mind goes back there now, there are
no roads going in or out. No way back remains because nothing is there, no continuation. Then life
itself, what is its worth to us? Why have we
bothered to live? All this is at an end. For myself, growing old would be altogether a different
thing if that little town was there still. All is
ended. So in my life, I carry with me everything
-- all those people, all those places, I carry
them around until my shoulders bend.

...Even with all that poverty and suffering, it
would be enough if the place remained, even old
men like me, ending their days, would find it
enough. But when I come back from these stories
and remember the way they lived is gone forever,
wiped out like you would erase a line of writing,
then it means another thing altogether to me to
accept leaving this life. If my life goes now,
it means nothing. But if my life goes, with my
memories, and all that is lost, that is something
else to bear.

The Life History Classes

Not long after I began my work in the Center, I began to
look for some appropriate means of reciprocating the Members
for the time they spent with me often talking about what I
wanted to learn. It was soon evident that providing them with
an opportunity to be heard, to recount their histories and

tell stories was ideal. This would constitute another arena
in which they could appear, in their own terms, and I would
serve as audience, conspicuously listening and documenting
what was said. I hoped also that some satisfaction would come
to them from listening to each other in formal circumstances,
that they would validate one another's accounts, and at the
same time stimulate and encourage each other's memories.
These hopes were fully realized in the form of a set of 'Living History' sessions, as the members called them. Members
were invited to attend "a class" that met for two hours or
more each week. The series ran five months, broke for the
summer and resumed for four months. Before long a rather
stable group of about twenty people formed itself and attended regularly.

     There were few rules. People were required to abstain
from interrupting each other. Everyone would have some time
to speak at each session, even briefly. Any content was acceptable. I reinforced the appropriateness of anyone's offerings, discouraging the Members from challenging the speak-
ers on matters of accuracy. The content discussed varied
greatly but loosely fell into four categories: Being Old,
Life in the Old Country, Being a Jew, Life in America. In
time, peoples' offerings grew more emotionally varied and less
guarded. They brought in dreams, recipes, questions about
ultimate concerns, folk remedies, book reports, daily logs
and the like. I encouraged them to keep journals, providing
notebooks and pens, and many did so with considerable pleasure.

     The Life History sessions paralleled the Definitional
Ceremonies in their presentational format. They were intended to persuade, and enactments were inserted as often as possible. Illustrations of points people wanted to make were
taken to class in the form of objects. They brought mementos,
gifts, plaques, awards, certificates, letters, publications,
and photographs from all periods of their and their families'
lives. One woman brought her sick husband who had grown se-
nile and could no longer speak coherently. She spoke for him,
recounting his stories, and along with them, the place he had
filled in her life. Another woman brought her retarded grand-
son "to show you what I am talking about when I tell you about
him." He was a kind of badge of honor, for she handled him
with dignity and patience, an injury transcended but for which
she wanted credit. Still another man brought in a yellow felt
star bearing the word "Jude." It circulated throughout the
room in silence. Words were not needed. The star dramatized
a major facet of his existence. A number of the women regularly brought in food, demonstrating their claimed skills as
cooks. Songs were sung, and from time to time there was

dancing. Poems were recited frequently in many languages,
demonstrations of erudition and memory. Learned quotations,
of Marx and Talmud, folk and fine literature also adorned
peoples' accounts. The sessions, then, were not merely verbal. Insofar as possible they were made into performances.
People displayed the qualities they wanted seen as much as
they could, and became what they displayed.

The importance of storytelling and a strong oral tradition among the Center members were significant factors in ac-
counting for the vitality of the Life History sessions.
Though profoundly literate, the oral tradition among Jews is
also highly developed, particularly in those exposed to
Hasidism. The recognition that words spoken aloud to another
person have particular power is a notion that weaves in and
out of Jewish culture. Shmuel spoke of the esteem for the
"wonder rebbes," the Hasidic teachers who travelled from one
town to another in Eastern Europe.

> Oh the stories they would tell us, full of wisdom,
> full of humor. It was immense. ...All of us,
> little boys by the dozens, would follow them when
> they came into the town. You could always tell
> them by the chalk on their caftans, this they car-
> ried to mark around them a circle of chalk that
> would keep out the spirits. My father did not ap-
> prove of me listening to them, but I would sneak
> out whenever I could, because what they brought
> you was absolutely magic. This experience was
> developing in me a great respect for telling
> stories. This is why it is important to get just
> the right attitude and just the right words for a
> story. You should get everything just right be-
> cause no matter how pleasant, it is a serious
> thing you are doing.

The sessions were not cosmetic. Catharsis occurred but
often more than that. Re-evaluations were clearly being
undertaken too. Having witnesses to this work proved essential. The elders found it hard to convince themselves of the
validity of their interpretations without some consensus from
the listeners. In time, they became better listeners. Though
they knew their audience of peers was going to die out with
them, members of the same generational cohorts have advantages as witnesses. They knew the reality being discussed
through direct experience. Less had to be explained and described to them, but the work of persuasion was often all the
more difficult because deception was less likely to be successful. When Jake quoted his father to demonstrate the latter's wisdom, one of the members promptly corrected him. "This

you are getting not from your father. It comes from Sholom
Aleichem." "And don't you think Sholom Aleichem learned anything from ordinary people?" he persisted. But no one was
impressed.

A story told aloud, to progeny or peers, is of course
more than a text. It is an event. When it is done properly,
presentationally, its effect on the listener is profound, and
the latter is more than a mere passive receiver or validator.
The listener is changed. This was recognized implicitly by
Rabbi Nachman of Bratzlav who ordered that all written records
of his teachings be destroyed. His words must be passed from
mouth to ear, learned by and in heart. "My words have no
clothes," he said. "When one speaks to one's fellows there
arises a simple light and a returning light." The impact of
the stories told by the old people to outsiders who would
stop to listen was consistently striking. Among those old
people embarked in the deep and serious work of Re-membering,
struggling toward self-knowledge and integration, it was especially clear that something important was going on. Sensitive young people, students and grandchildren, often found
themselves fascinated by the old people's life histories. The
sociological shibboleth that claims in a rapidly changing
society the elderly have nothing more to teach must be recon-
sidered. Anyone in our times struggling toward wholeness,
self-knowledge based on examined experience, and clarity about
the worth of the enterprise exerts a great attraction on those
searching for clarity. In the company of elders such as these,
listeners perform an essential service. But they get more
than they give, and invariably grow from the contact.

When the sessions were at their best, the old people were
conscious of the importance of their integration work, not
only for themselves but for posterity, however modestly represented. Then they felt the high satisfaction of being able
to fulfill themselves as individuals as Exemplars of a tradition at once. Then they were embodiments of the shared meanings -- true Ancestors -- as well as individuals in full possession of their past. Rachel described such a moment most
eloquently when she talked about what the sessions had meant
to her.

All these speeches we are making reminded me of a
picture I have from many years ago, when we were
still in Russia. My brother had been gone already
two years in America. I can see my mother like it
is before me, engraved in my head. A small house
she goes out of in wintertime, going every morning

in the snow to the post office, wrapped up in a
shawl. Every morning there was nothing. Finally,
she found a letter. In that letter was written,
"Mamalch, I didn't write to you before because I
didn't have nothing to write about." "So," she
says, "why didn't you write and tell me?"

You know this group of ours reminds me of that
letter. When I first heard about this group, I
thought to myself, "What can I learn? What can I
hear that I don't know, about life in the Old
Country, of the struggles, the life in the poor
towns, in the bigger towns, of the rich people and
the poor people? What is there to learn, I'm
eighty-eight, that I haven't seen myself?" Then I
think, "What can I give to anybody else? I'm not
an educated woman. It's a waste of time."

That was my impression. But then I came here and
heard all those stories. I knew them, but you
know it was laid down deep, deep in your mind,
with all those troubles mixed. You know it's
there but you don't think of it, because sometimes
you don't want to live in your past. Who needs
all these foolish stories?

But finally, this group brought out such beautiful memories, not always so beautiful, but still
all the pictures came up. It touched the layers
of the kind that it was on those dead people already. It was laying on them like layers, separate layers of earth, and all of a sudden in this
class I feel it coming up like lava. It just
melted away the earth from all those people. It
melted away, and they became alive. And then to
me it looked like they were never dead.

Then I felt like the time my mother got that
letter. "Why don't you come and tell me?" "Well,
I have nothing to say," I think. But I start to
say it and I find something. The memories come
up in me like lava. So I felt I enriched myself.
And I am hoping maybe I enriched somebody else.
All this, it's not only for us. It's for the
generations.

Acknowledgements

Special thanks are due to Victor and Edith Turner, Richard Schechner and Alexander Alland, whose seminar on "Performance and Anthropology" at the Drama Department of New York University in June, 1979 provided information and inspiration for many of the ideas discussed here. The 1977 Wenner-Gren Foundation conference co-convened by the author and Barbara Babcock on "Cultural Frames and Reflections: Ritual, Drama and Spectacle" was a critical event in developing some of my interpretations of reflexivity. Gelya Frank provided stimulation and generously shared references and ideas. Naturally, only I am responsible for the views given here.

References

1.   "The Problem of Generations," in Paul Kecskemeti, ed., Essays in the Sociology of Knowledge, London: Routledge, Kegan and Paul, p. 290, (no date).

2.   Tamara K. Hareven, "The Search for Generational Memory: Tribal Rites in Industrial Society," in Daedalus: Journal of the American Academy of Arts and Sciences, Special Issue on 'Generations,' Fall, 1978, pp. 137-149.

3.   Charlotte Linde distinguishes between 'narrative' that implies an evaluative dimension and 'chronicle,' a list of events that does not imply evaluation. See Charlotte Linde, "The Creation of Coherence in Life Stories" (April, 1978; available from Structural Semantics, P.O. Box 5612, Santa Monica, California, 90405).

4.   Clifford Geertz speaks of ritual as "the fusion of the dreamed-of and lived-in order," in "Religion as a Cultural System," in Anthropological Approaches in the Study of Religion, edited by M. Banton. New York: Praeger, 1965.

Suzanne Langer uses the term "virtual power" in discussing the capacity of symbols to arouse the imagination and provide an experience of a convincing though invisible reality. See Suzanne K. Langer, Philosophy in a New Key. Cambridge: Harvard University Press, 1960.

5.   Langer, op. cit.

6.   For a fuller discussion of the capacity of ritual to redefine social relationships see Sally Falk Moore and Barbara G. Myerhoff, "Introductions: Forms and Meanings," in Secular Ritual, Amsterdam: Van Gorcum, 1977, Moore and Myerhoff (eds.).

7.   This notion is derived from Victor Turner's concept of "Social Dramas," but used somewhat differently; this is discussed in Myerhoff's Number Our Days.

8.   Robert Jay Lifton, Death in Life: Survivors of Hiroshima, New York: Simon and Schuster, 1967.

9.   Cited in The Philosophy of Wilhelm Dilthey, by H.A. Hodges, London: Routledge, Kegan and Paul, 1952, pp. 274-275.

10.   Adam A. Mendilow, Time and Experience, London: Peter Nevill, 1952, p. 137.

11.   See especially Erikson's discussion of old age in "Reflections on Dr. Borg's Life Cycle," in Adulthood, Erik Erikson editor, New York: W.W. Norton, 1978, pp. 1-31.

12.   Sigmund Freud, Death, Grief and Mourning, New York: Doubleday, 1965.

13.   Vladimir Nabokov, Speak Memory: An Autobiography Revisited, New York: G.P. Putnam's Sons, 1966, p. 21.

14.   Elie Wiesel, Messengers of God: Biblical Portraits and Legends, translated by Marion Wiesel, New York: Vintage Books, 1973.

15.   Ms. Sack presented her work-in-progress (not yet titled) to a session of the seminar on 'Performance and Anthropology', conducted by Richard Schechner at New York University, June, 1979.

Part 3

Conclusion

9. Mathematics and the Poetry of Human Life and Points In-Between

The Language of the Life Course

The course of human life is both the most personal and the most universal event which we know. The life cycle, with its predetermined and ineluctable order of occurrences, forms a framework in which we perceive all other events. In its basic scheme - birth, growth, maturity, decline and death - we know that it is universal for all our fellow humans. However, as an experience, each feels the course of his own life to be unique.

The relationship between individual lives and social process is difficult to discern. It seems to be easier to establish patterns and to make predictions for aggregates of people rather than for individuals. Statistical distributions are more easily obtained for aggregates, and in the social sciences, methods are generally more established and better adapted for dealing with groups than for tracing the lives of individuals. The methods developed for studying an individual life as a whole are still rudimentary and look more like a confluence of methods from different disciplines than a foundation for a discipline in its own right.

Scientific specialties have taken a part of human life and dissected it, such as in studies of childhood, adolescence, gerontology, and lately, even studies of adult life. Or they look at different aspects of life - as in the study of developmental physiology, embryology, psychology, or social development. For those studies that concentrate only on social development, the primary scientific investigation extends only to certain aspects of human life. One talks about family or work roles, or intellectual life, or community and political life, sometimes about interaction and conflict.

In taking on the human life course as a unit, we must transcend the temporal division of life into different stages, and to combine the different role-set within the space of the society, to find the unique lives for their whole course. Combining the many possibilities within one human life into one unit needs a special skill, having something of art and something of science. It is no wonder therefore, that we have so many different ways to tackle the story of human lives. Different points of view and different languages can deal partially with the task of prescribing the unity of the individual within the biological and social framework, and reducing the wealth of variables to comprehensible statements.

Developments in physics have frequently been cited as an analogy. On a micro-level we cannot predict the path of an individual particle, but the laws of physics on the macro-level are well established, based on the probability distributions of the actions of the particle. The impossibility of making exact statements about sub-atomic particles has been established as a formal law of nature - Heisenberg's Principle of Indeterminacy. This principle is frequently invoked as a proof that conventional social research on individuals is impossible. Although a simple analogy is dangerous and unwarranted here, it may be that modern physics has worked out a solution to its own problem that can be applicable to the social scientist's efforts to deal alternately with the carpiciousness of individual fate and the regularity of social events in determining a model of the life course.

In applying this analogy, we have to decide on the position of the individual. Is one human life analogous to one particle as represented in sociological research or to the macro-level of many attitudes and actions, which is the psychological perspective. Thus it is almost up to the investigator to decide whether the human life course is so small as to constitute random behavior, so large as to be beyond comprehension or legitimate research, or whether it is the ideal subject matter for scientific investigation.

The framework for the study of the life course is usually not chosen purposively by the scientist. The disciplinary point of view taken determines the aspects which are selected and neglected and the kinds of statements which can be made. The selection of language is made prior to any actual scientific work, the possible approaches are predetermined in the orientation of the society, in the perceptions and beliefs which are permissible and which are possible to be exposed. No particular language can encompass

all of experience. The totality of human life cannot be
encompassed in any language. Some of the intensities are
ineffable.

The object of this paper is to uncover the possibilities
of a point of view which tries to express the role of the
individual and the means to encompass it. To again take
recourse in our analogy from physics, Heisenberg's Principle,
this means that we may ascertain either the position or the
momentum of a particle depending on the experiment we design.
Thus we have not only an analogy between the particles of
physics and the individuals in a social field; the two areas
are intimately connected, and, in the language of the psychologist, the nature of the subject matter depends on the figure-
ground relationship of the observer. The very entity of a
human life course may be a human creation rather than a fact
of nature. As early as the nineteenth century, Schopenhauer
compared the persistent idea of human fate with the workings
of an anamorphic conical mirror which creates human figures
out of disconnected fragments (1). The kind of mirror which
we use to emphasize or de-emphasize human lives is part of
our cultural and personal disposition. Another analogy which
might be of use from the history of physics is that the choice
of a model is ultimately an aesthetic choice (2).

We shall look first at the whole range of methods and
language which can treat the human life. This includes the
work of the poet as well as the work of the sociologist. We
shall see that to surmount the temptation to deal with only
part of life, we shall need new languages. Joyce's Ulysses
can be seen as the way in which a poet can deal with this
task. Finally, we can sketch, on the other extreme, a
mathematical language adequate to this challenge.

Myth

The myths of a society are expressions of its pre-language
orientation. Mythology combines interpretations of the
natural world, its connections with the social world, a view
of the life course and a framework built on the history of
society itself, in an intrinsic pattern that single verbal
descriptions cannot cope with. Myths are typically stories
about a hero whose life stages represent the organization of
the basic beliefs of the people. The myth then represents
a fundamental figure-ground relation in the social language.
Encompassing the whole of experience, it stresses certain
aspects of life and puts others into the background.

A new theme entered mythology in the medieval Arthurian
romances, namely the idea of an individual self-made destiny.

Heroes before that time, and heroes in non-European myths,
live out their destinies, dependent on individual position,
prophecies and their significance as representatives. The
individual hero, who does not follow destiny, and can change
his character and defy prophecies, comes into the myth at this
time, especially in the figure of Parzifal, and to a lesser
degree, Tristam and Isolde, and other Arthurian characters (3).
The individual becomes the main figure, and society, nature
and their forces become background. Individual reality
accompanied the myth. Heloise, and, up to a point, Abelard,
are the early representatives of modern individuals, fighting
and managing their fate. This individualism has now pervaded
our own background to such an extent that it is hard to see
it as a pattern of and out on our organization of human
sciences (4). The importance of the human life course, seen
as a unit, is an achievement of Western civilization. It
allowed the perception of a new unit of the individual life,
distinct from social rules and short time slices, family, the
discovery of world of objects, the experiences of the social
group and the achievement of one's own status, to the impact
of old age and death. The mythology of different peoples
reflects their own culture, their history, and their circumstances; but in each myth we can find the convergence of the
universal fate of development and the individual experience
of realizing a specific set of circumstances.

The prevailing myth will find expression in the society
through its conventional language. In our scientific society
this means the different disciplines. Calls for interdisciplinary work reflect the need for transcending this
restriction to specific codes, while re-emphasis on progress
in particular disciplines accepts the advantage of a self-
consistent language system. In looking for a proper language
for the topic of the human life course, we shall first
examine a range of approaches which may provide the right
combination and then look at the probabilities of integration
by taking aim from the two extreme positions.

Myths cannot be consciously created; they must correspond
to social beliefs. They can be expressed - and modify in
expression - in societies expressions. A humanistic approach
to human life may look for a science of the life course in a
set of symbols acceptable today, in contemporary language.
Creative artistic work, such as a drama, a novel or a poem,
concentrates on one central incident which tries to illuminate
the life of a character to such a degree that all the character's previous and subsequent actions become consistent and
reasonable. The emphasis on the style and form of the artist
makes these productions intuitively valid, as contributions
to the study of the human life course, but the language used

in each individual work is so idiosyncratic to the artist that
we can hardly speak of method, certainly not of a method which
can be expounded.

Biography and Poetry

Biographies are humanistic expressions centering on the
life course, using a definite set of rules of evidence.
Biographies have, in fact, been called "novels under oath."
They are attempts to create unity in the wealth of facts which
it is possible to obtain about one person. This is done, not
by selection of a few manipulatable variables, but by an act
of artistic creation. "Biography is a work of the imagination
--the imagination of form and style and narrative. The biographer is allowed to be as imaginative as he pleases, as
long as he does not imagine his facts" (5). Biography involves
a unified picture of life, which is not synthesized by other
methods.

It may inappropriate here to talk about methodology in
biography in the same way we discuss psychological and
sociological methods. Biography in this sense involves more
the genius of the biographer than a codifiable method which
can be applied for large-scale comparisons. Certainly,
techniques in finding and evaluating sources of data, in
assembling material and in assessing contradictory evidence
can be taught like any sociological methodology. But, as
Edel says in the same article, adherence only to these rules
produces a "compendium-life...the work of a journeyman of
letters" (5).

Thus, biography depends on the individual style of the
author, not on the accumulation of data. Lytton Strachey,
one of the founders of modern biography, made brevity, the
elimination of non-essential facts, the essence of good
biography (6). Scientific approaches really work by elimination of what they consider unessential but from a different
point of view. We have here two contrasts: elimination
simply by adhering to one principle or one discipline -
e.g., psychoanalytic biography or sociological life goals
study, and the manner of selection by the intuition of the
humanist and the disciplinary rules of the scientist. In
both contrasts we find a competition between perception in
description of actions and appreciation of human uniqueness.
Perhaps this is the old contrast between art and science,
coming together in the need of a precise definition of the
self.

For the poet, the self is the unique character; understanding the self and discovering it means trying to state

the unique in general terms, to express the ineffable in a way
that can be understood by others. Thus, in effect, presenting
the self in language becomes an impossible task, defined by
the two incompatible terms of ineffability and communication.
In the metaphor that the existentialists use, the more we get
to the core of the self, the less we find, and being, which
is everything, becomes nothingness. Here is the problem of
the humanist or the poet in trying to describe the whole of
life.

The Scientist

A corresponding problem faces the social scientist. In
order to translate events into mathematics, the ideal language
of science, we have to concentrate on the measurable, visible
effects of human life, that is, decisions whose consequences
can be perceived. We have to simplify the decisions and take
only those aspects of each which are measurable - a decision
may be taken on the basis of either a simple yes or no, or it
may be taken only to a certain degree. The self so defined
becomes identified with just some of its aspects. In the
context of life development, the self can be related to some
stage of life such as age, or some aspect of personal worth,
such as self-concept or self-esteem, or some social characteristic such as income, work or education.

The artist as well as the scientist has struggled to find
an appropriate form with which to encompass the life course.
By comparing the achievements of each discipline, how each -
art as well as science - has attempted with its own limited
resources, to represent the whole life course, we can find
guidelines for a future theory.

Jacob Bronowski (7), in comparing art and science, joins
the two through the concept of the artifact. An artifact is
intensely and uniquely human and we may ask of it questions
in two directions: How was it made? and what is it for?
Language, which is an artifact in itself, lends itself to the
same questions. In scientific language, whose purpose is
prediction and control, we are told how conclusions are
reached. In poetic language we can also objectively analyze
as critics or linguists how certain poetic effects are
produced. This leads us to a greater understanding of the
poetic art. However, here the relationship between the
reader and the poem is more immediate - what we have learned
about poetry is not something which then enables us to write
our own; rather, the meaning of the poem has become part of
ourselves.

This contrast becomes extremely important if we want to
explain the whole of human life. Here we can look at unique

phenomena as immediate experiences which shape the inner life
of each person and have to be transmitted through language
which arouses the same emotions in others. We can also look
at public phenomena and reproduce them in a special language,
which can be applied to a variety of people. This is scientific
language, and a scientific description of biographies is a
study of decisions; going from one decision point to the next,
we can investigate a sequence of decisions, and the relationships between them, and build up in that way a kind of life
cycle. This task of the developmental theorists, be they
psychologists or sociologists, adds up from decision point to
decision point. From schooling to leaving home to first job
to marriage, having children and finally, the various stages
of dissolution of relationships during old age - these choice
points describe the parameters of demography as well as of the
social psychology of development and of achievement; they
define a person's position in a personal or social space.

     With some justification, many people claim that this is
not all of what we know of human life. They are supported
by the biographer and the novelist, who try to fill out the
missing parts, the transitions between the different decisions
- the real meaning which these experiences have for the
individual. There are different ways to do this. There is
the dramatic moment in which one decision compresses the
whole life of the character into the smallest possible space
or time. There is the representative anecdote of the biographer which tries to illuminate the life of a character
through some insightful action or exchange. There is the
direct appeal of the allusions of a poem which attempt
to enter into the immediacy of real life experience, through
some insight into human existence. All of these artistic
devices try to capture the flow of life, its time span, rather
than focussing merely on decisions and their consequences,
their public and observable outcomes.

Two Extremes

     Thus both the artist and the scientist chafe under the
restrictions of language. To discuss the self, which vanishes
when it is too closely contemplated, as well as the life
cycle, which encompasses all of experience, the normal language of the artist as well as that of the scientist is, as
we have said, insufficient. As a challenge to the scientist,
let us look at one example of the transcendence of language
in which an artist took up the task of depicting the full
dimension of human life in one fell swoop.

     James Joyce in Ulysses tried to compress in the story of
one man's day the meaning of the historical development of
man, his achievements, legends, myths, stressing the

importance of the human body as a representation of one human
life and, thus, by extension, the human life of every man.
He did this by transcending the ordinary forms of the novel,
of the narrative as well as of ordinary language. He used
archaic language as well as allusions, his own encyclopedic
knowledge, new words which he coined, puns, experiments in
style, parodies, imitations, a variety of traditional and
newly invented linguistic devices. The novel seems at first
glance to be loose, undisciplined, self-indulgent and impossible
to comprehend. On another level, it gives the reader a pure
enjoyment of words, of their sounds and of their grammar. Or,
one can merely enjoy the sequence of scenes, given at least
a vague idea of the thread of the story. Beyond this, closer
inspection reveals an almost overly rigid structure and an
exact design which is missing from other ostensibly more
organized stories. The eighteen chapters of the novel represent well-bounded times and locations in the story to be told
as well as corresponding scenes in the myth of Ulysses on
which Joyce's work is, to some extent, based. In addition,
each chapter represents an aspect of the human mind and body,
as well as a symbol, a human art, an organ, a color, and,
especially, a different technique of language. Thus a chapter
in the novel which describes a visit to a newspaper office,
and in the myth of Ulysses the Cave of the Winds, celebrates
the human achievement of rhetoric; it also includes all the
possible devices which the Greek rhetoricians have listed as
decorating persuasive speech. Similarly, a visit to an
obstetrics hospital represents the mythological aspect of the
Oxen of the Sun, a symbol of fertility. It also celebrates
the growth of language and literature, parallel to the events
taking place in the chapter (in the Lying-in Hospital). In
addition, to properly illustrate the theme of the development
of language, the chapter is written in a shifting style
starting with that of the first English grammars and moving
through the whole of English literature up to Joyce's own
time, using a few paragraphs to parody or imitate the style
of each period. Looked at in this way, the language of
Ulysses is over-determined. Each word, each sentence of each
page has to follow so many functions that it seems to have
been put into position with an almost scientific precision.
Joyce attempts in this way to combine the outward actions of
the characters with their inner experience, the stream of
consciousness. We can see now why the normal novelistic
language was not sufficient to carry all these meanings.

The invention of a new language was seen at first glance
as an abstruse conceit. We can see on further deliberation
that it is a grandiose attempt at facing the impossibility
of expressing the ineffable character of the self. As such
it is a great achievement and it remains a challenge to us.

Geometry of the Life Course

But what can we do on the side of social science to
contrive a scientific language capable of dealing with the
complexities of the human life course? Clearly, we have to
construct a mathematics which will encompass human life from
a scientific perspective as effectively as Joyce did from an
interior one. It will be a new mathematics quite different
from what we have understood as classic mathematics, one
which will perhaps be incomprehensible to us even as we are
working on it.

A social scientist, describing the regularities of human
life, cannot write a description of data using Joyce's multi-
faceted language. However, he does not have to be bound by
the mathematical conventions into which we have fallen in
order to analyze the observable universe of a process such
as that of decision-making. The basis of the language used
to express these data is arithmetic: We count the individuals
before they make a decision according to certain characteristics,
such as social status, sex, ethnicity, education, and then
we classify people according to the decisions they actually
make, e.g., which occupation they choose. The rules of data
analysis are clear and definite: each number represents the
definite procedure by which it has been obtained, each
statistical method - cross-tabulation, correlation, regression
- gives a definite set of numbers which describe the relations
of the frequencies. This clarity may be more apparent than
real, however. The term called "error" can be very large and
it represents the ineffable, that which we cannot talk about.
Furthermore, the most complicated structure really encompasses
only a small part of life. Models may represent occupational
achievement, longevity, fertility or income, but rarely any
combination of these. The results obtained in this way are
the building blocks of a theory of human life. They are
necessary and compact, but they lack a general, overall design.

A design for the life course starts with some ideas on its
structure and meaning. In designing a model of the life
course, there are problems - like Joyce, whose intention was
to give an idea of the multiplicity of thoughts that make up
human consciousness at any one moment, we have too many
determinations for each human act and each sequence of acts.
Only by denying the multiplicity of influences as well as
of events acting on each individual can we reduce our findings
to the simple numbers which are frequently the outcomes of
social research. However, if we should take into account the
range of influences, the ambiguities of meaning and the
different social structures which impinge on each life, the
set of equations and variables would then become too large and

and unwieldy to be handled or interpreted. The language
of mathematics, the language which we are to use, must
correspond to the subtle shadings and multiplicities of
meaning of the subject matter which we want to represent.

Computer scientists who tried to represent intelligent
behavior were among the first who faced this aspect of the
mathematics of human behavior. The nature of intelligent
behavior - as the nature of experience in the life course -
lies in the fact that the units under discussion are not
determined; new uses can be invented for familiar objects,
new combinations can be tried out, and obscure similarity
can be used, a leap into the unknown can be based on
insufficient evidence. The indeterminancy of the data
representing intelligent behavior does not stem from any
weakness in measurement. The units of thought which lead to
intelligent behavior are not definite themselves. Representing
them in crisp, neat sets and functions would eliminate exactly
those aspects which make them useful for intelligent behavior;
this is their adaptability to different configurations until
the best fit is discovered.

Scientists working on Artificial Intelligence developed
therefore a new branch of mathematics, namely that of fuzzy
subsets (7). Membership in fuzzy subsets is by degrees; it
can be used, for example, to define the terms of ordinary
language. Different ages have membership in the set of "old
people"; 80 has almost perfect membership, 60 to a considerable
degree, 40 to a low degree, and 20 is practically excluded.
We can also define commitment to particular roles in the
same way: membership in a role set is really a fuzzy
variable - it is not well defined by the nature of the
concept, and attempts at exact measurement only falsify the
situation. We can make rules about the combination of these
different life structures and the satisfactions inherent in
each role and define persons by their involvement in these
different membership sets as well as their attraction to them.

We can then talk about individuals with respect to their
similarity to each other, and we can develop new ideas about
different kinds of similarity which might not have occurred
to us before. Like Joyce, whose linguistic inventions were
necessary to represent the concept of "stream of consciousness,"
social scientists must construct a new vocabulary and new
syntactical rules with which to define the meaning of the life
course, such as stream of attitudes or stream of behavior.

We can also note that the representation of these fuzzy
sets is more natural in a geometry of forms than in the
arithmetic of numbers. The different shadings and functions

of fuzzy sets give a more faithful picture of one particular
part of life than its determination by a set of numbers.

We can thus analyze a number of variables for individuals
at different points of time. The first step is to develop
clusters which are both synchronous and diachronic, combining
a number of variables over some part of the life span. After
these clusters have been defined, we can establish a trace for
each person, the change from one cluster to another over
different stages of life. By introducing fuzzy clusters we
can add a refinement, adding degrees of membership. Then we
can establish points of meaningful breaks in the life course,
where membership in one cluster cannot be maintained.

To analyze the changes we take our techniques from biological development (8). Progress of an embryo proceeds quite
regularly and is stable within limits, until certain definite
stages occur, such as the development of different kinds of
cells. What we need here is not a minute consideration gradual
changes, but a determination of the large-scale qualitative
changes of the curves,their definition and classification.
Such questions have led to a new branch of geometry and
topology which is commonly called catastrophe theory after its
most prominent feature, the discontinuous change. In the
study of the life course, the catastrophes correspond to the
decision points, the events of life visible to the outsider.
Mathematically, catastrophes occur at certain unstable points
in a family of curves when a small change may greatly alter
the shape of a curve (as defined by its maxima and minima).
Psychologically, we may call these crisis points, points
where small inputs may lead to great change. We can determine
these points according to their presence in population groups,
as well as such unusual occurrences in individual lives. These
techniques are therefore applicable to population as well as
to individual analyses.

Conclusion

The geometrical theories which I have outlined give us a
mathematical framework in which to fit the few data points
which we can obtain for human lives. They give us long
stretches of stable situations, which can be described as a
long stream of consciousness. Descriptions of consciousness,
whether given by Freud or by Joyce, show a curious kind of
stability: there is variation from point to point, but the
general thrust remains relatively constant. This constancy
can be defined by geometrical methods, such as that of fuzzy
sets. These methods can then describe unique private states,
which refer only to one individual. The large changes, which
go beyond any definition of stability, can be analyzed by the

principles of catastrophe theory: they may seem too obvious
to need the mechanisms of such a heavy mathematical theory,
but they can provide a framework in which to fit the public
data which we are able to obtain.

Each human life is a unique curve, defined by its important determinants. Some are similar enough to form, grouped
together, what are called families of curves, distinguished
only by individual parameters, which we may call personality
or social background. Shifts in these curves may be sudden
and extreme reorganizations, which represent real crises, or
they may be just apparent shifts, within a regular curve,
which are unreal crises. The combination and classification
of these forms can become a science of the life course.

The preceding sketch of current geometrical innovations
discusses what may seem to be cumbersome techniques for social
research. The problem, however, may be simpler than we think:
the advantage of the poet, of the biographer, of the mytho-
logist has always been his ability to give form to human life
which is more impressive than any mass of numerical data.
Those attempting to give form to the efforts of social
scientists may have to learn to combine bare facts with the
insights of poetry.

References

1. Schopenhauer, A., Transcendent Speculation on the Apparent
    Deliberateness in the Fate of the Individual, in Parerga
    and Paralipomena, (Oxford, Oxford University Press, 1974,
    originally published 1851), 199-223.

2. Miller, D. I. Visualization Lost and Regained: The Genesis
    of Quantum Theory in the Period 1913-27.

3. Campbell, J. The Masks of God: Creative Mythology,
    Viking, New York, 1968.

4. Sampson, E. E., Psychology and the American Ideal,
    Journal of Personality and Social Psychology, 35, 1977,
    767-82.

5. Edell, L. Biography: A Manifesto, Biography, 1, 1978,
    1-3.

6. Strachey, L. Emminent Victorians, Introduction, London,
    1918, Chatto and Winduz.

7. Bronowski, J. The Visionary Eye, MIT Press, Cambridge,
    Mass., 1978.

8. Kaufmann, A. <u>Fuzzy Set Theory</u>, 1973, Marmon, Paris, eighth edition, Academic Press, 1977.

9. Thom, R. <u>Stabilite Structurell et Morphogenes</u>, Benjamin, New York, 1972, English edition, 1975.

Index